COMING HOME

COMING HOME

The Return to True Self

Martia Nelson

In gratitude,
and loving memory of
my mother, Virginia,
Mrs. Tate, and
painter extraordinaire, Letty Pang

With love and pets to
Chloe and Rincon

ACKNOWLEDGMENTS

I extend my heartfelt gratitude to Marilyn Hughes for friendship and unwavering encouragement for my work and this book; Jan Fischer for insightful editing and gracious delivery; Sarah Francis for making my computer seem almost friendly, and Linda Thomas for providing years of safe harbor to my insecurity about sharing myself with the world.

I am honored that my longtime friend and gifted book cover designer Gaelyn Larrick designed this cover, and that artist Jesse Reisch "got" me and created the perfect art piece for it.

Shakti Gawain, thank you for first publishing *Coming Home* in 1993 and for your timeless friendship. You are family.

To all who choose a path of true self discovery: I am grateful to be traveling with you.

CONTENTS

NOTE: Except where last names are given, names used in the stories
    are not people's real names.

ATTUNEMENTS AND MEDITATIONS

To make the material as practical and usable as possible, attunements and guided meditations are sprinkled throughout this book. For quick reference, they are listed below. As you work with these suggestions, let yourself be creative in altering them to fit your needs and your sense of truth.

PREFACE

I've known Martia Nelson for many years. I've watched her go through the evolutionary process she describes in the first part of this book, and I've seen her develop an extraordinary connection with inner guidance as she writes about in Part II. I've had intuitive reading from her over the years, and received amazingly clear and accurate insights and advice.

When Martia sent me the original version of this manuscript, I stayed up almost all night reading it, feeling very excited. I knew it was one of the best metaphysical books I had ever read.

Coming Home is a clear, practical and inspiring explanation of how we can integrate our human experience with our essential spiritual nature and express the potential that dwells within all of us. As I read it, it actually lifts me into an expanded perspective on my life. I have found it very helpful in my own personal process, and I know others will as well. Anyone who has resonated with my work is likely to love this book.

Frankly, at this stage of my life I read very few books of this nature. This one will be on my bedside table for quite some time. I believe it's destined to become a classic.

—Shakti Gawain

INTRODUCTION

We all know what it's like to want to improve ourselves. We want to be loving, patient, and compassionate. To be better parents and better people...learn to forgive...develop our creative gifts...find meaning in life as we bring peace and goodness to the world...and become spiritually evolved, or even enlightened. These are wonderful things to want!

And there are situations in our outer lives we wish would improve, too. We want a job doing something we love, something that makes our heart sing and our soul soar. We want more money so we can feel safe and supported and free. We want a relationship with a true partner, a soul mate who will help us open to our full capacity to love and be loved. We want to release the struggle in our lives and replace it with harmony and balance. In short, we want to thrive!

We are ready to make the shift from surviving to thriving.

This book can help us do that. I wrote it from my heart, knowing that most of us struggle with a split between our personality (everyday identity, or ego) and spirit (infinite source, or true self) without recognizing what this struggle is or how it holds us back. This split is the rift in our awareness that keeps us overly identified with the material world and out of touch with our inherent spiritual nature. It keeps us unfulfilled, better at surviving than thriving.

Because our culture doesn't teach us about the split, we often don't realize the personal crises it creates. Usually the distress begins on such a subtle level that we barely feel it at first. We have vague feelings that something is missing from our lives. We feel burned out at our jobs or dissatisfied with our relationships, but we shrug it off. Something always happens that keeps us from having enough money. Or we have money, but it doesn't make us happy. Or deep down, unexpressed creativity is pushing to get free, but we tell ourselves we will find an outlet for it "later". Maybe we can't even identify what is bothering us—we long for something more, but what?

The distress of our inner split builds over the years to a point of crisis. Health problems may surface. Relationships may crumble. Financial stress may overwhelm us. We may feel trapped in our jobs or panicked about retirement. We suffer a loss that we think we can't cope with. As we witness violence in the world, we feel perpetually unsafe. Or, even after all we've done and accomplished over the decades, life lacks meaning. As we get older our fear of death may creep closer. A growing suspicion that we haven't developed our greater potential or made our most meaningful contribution to the world yet—and fear that we may run out of time to live a wholly fulfilled life—can start dulling our days and keeping us up at night. Or we can no longer ignore a perennial loneliness that remains unsoothed by the relationships and accomplishments in our lives so far.

Even if we don't understand why these crises are occurring, they are signs that we're at a turning point. We're ready to discover a reality greater than we ever thought possible. In fact, we sense that we *need* this discovery, that we can't keep going the same way we have in the past.

Because this greater reality is still unidentified *potential* to us, not yet real to our intellect or five senses, we may vacillate between being drawn to it and doubting its existence. We may sometimes think we're making it up, that we should drop it and go back to our old ways. But we can't. Even if we're seasoned spiritual seekers who have made profound breakthroughs already, we now crave the next, more expansive level of spiritual awakening. We feel a pull, and we have to follow it.

The pull is from our true self. True self is our source, the essence of our very being, our spirit. In fact, it is the spirit that we, and all things and all beings, are made of. Because true self is the material and intelligence of all creation, including us, it connects us with all creation and offers us everything we want most, including unconditional love and unlimited well-being. It holds back nothing from us and asks nothing in return.

True self is with us at all times because it *is* us, yet we've lived most of our lives oblivious to it. Perhaps we have glimpsed it for brief periods but have been unable to sustain that awareness through the nitty gritty of our lives. It becomes easier to recognize, trust, and feel supported by true self if we learn how to direct our awareness to it—and if we are willing to adopt a kinder, more compassionate and inclusive view of ourselves, others, and the world. It's important that we do this. Our individual lives, as well as the world, are going through such change and facing such challenge that we need true self's expansive perspective to bring healing to ourselves and to our planet.

In the pages ahead, beginning with my own story of awakening to true self, I share perceptions and techniques for living consciously in the greater reality of true self. This book is designed to help us identify, love, and integrate the two realities our culture has held separate: personality and true self.

By embracing the personality, yet also expanding beyond it
to the unlimited love, guidance, and creative power of true self,
we can thrive.

Coming Home was first published in 1993. To make the spiritual concepts even more practical and usable, this edition contains updates absent in editions earlier than 2010—plus more information about two subjects I love: Sounding (using vocal sounds to open to true self) and the Nothing (or void, or emptiness). I also have continued *My Story* to include you in the surprising journey true self orchestrated for me between 1993 and 2010.

In the *Self-Love* chapter I have added one of my favorite true self tools, a process I call *Sweet Me*. I developed it several years ago, and it has become one of my most effective tools for helping people to reach easily and gently beyond the personality's habituated patterns of suffering to tap the unwavering compassion and well-being of true self. I have begun writing a new book about Sweet Me, and I am happy to be sharing some of it here so you can start using it.

In *Creating Your World: Abundance and Manifesting*, I talk about the natural flow of abundance and our participation with it. In recent years there has been a bursting forth of information about the law of attraction and other abundance practices, including the following concepts: *Like attracts like. We attract people, things, and circumstances that match our vibration. Our outer state is a reflection of our inner state. The secret to creating outer abundance is creating an inner state of abundance. We can magnetize to us the things we want by using affirmations, visualization, and gratitude. Feeling the joy of already having the things we want can hasten those things to us.*

I agree with and am inspired by a great deal of the abundance material I come across—but often there is an omission of one element I consider to be essential because, to me, it is the *foundation* of the law of attraction and abundance practices in general: true self. You might choose a different term than true self (perhaps Spirit, God, higher self, Source, or something that feels more personally meaningful to you).

I think true self (or your term for spirit) needs to be center stage in abundance practice because it is the source of all abundance. An abundance practice that does not engage us with spirit is likely to yield limited, and very temporary, results. Most significantly, the abundance we receive from that practice will not give us the unwavering well-being we thought it would.

> *True self is our being at the level of creation,*
> *where the abundance we seek already exists*
> *and everything already is available to us.*

In true self we *are* abundance. We *are* spirit and creation. We *are* the source we hope will respond to our abundance-based affirmations, visualization, and gratitude.

Another way to look at it is that we don't have to create an inner state of abundance at all—we can simply drop into the one we already have in our true self! Our personality believes in and experiences lack; our true self *is* abundance. Giving our personality tools for recognizing and experiencing true self abundance opens us to the abundant world we long for but have been missing. To me, the beauty of an abundance practice is that our personality becomes aware that it is co-creating with true self—and is held in the embrace of true self while doing it!

The personality directs our instinct for surviving;
true self carries our blueprint for thriving.

As you open to yourself in a new way while reading this book, emotions may occasionally surface that you have not yet fully explored or maybe didn't even know were there. If this happens, take good care of yourself, and get the support you need. You might want to talk to close friends or to a pastoral counselor such as a minister or rabbi. You might consider joining a support group or finding a good therapist who can guide you through your feelings. Be sensitive to your needs. Getting comfort and support from trustworthy sources during times of change is essential. I mention this periodically throughout the book because it is important. Having a well cared for and healthy personality that feels nurtured and safe enables you to stabilize amidst rapid growth and to open to deeper levels of spiritual experience.

To help you put new information to practical use, I have provided meditations and what I call *attunements* throughout the book. The attunements are ways to direct your awareness as you go about your day—ways that you can tune into a deeper reality even as you remain at your everyday level of consciousness. The meditations are intended for times when you can take several minutes and allow yourself a longer period of inner exploration without being involved in any activity. Feel free to personalize these attunements and meditations, using your own wording, imagery, or personal focus.

Some of the material in this book will touch you deeply. As you read each chapter, I encourage you to write down any insights or Aha's while they are fresh. They are likely to be meaningful to you for years to come.

To get the richest, juiciest benefit from the book, I suggest forming a *Coming Home* reading group so you can discuss it chapter-by-chapter with like-minded folks who share your interest in personal growth and spiritual unfolding. The discussion can enhance your understanding of the information presented here and help you apply it more deeply to your life—as well as give you group support for living from your true self.

Group support is a powerful resource. As you will read in the *Journey into Form* chapter, we began losing our awareness of true self early in life as we adapted to groups of people: family, friends, school, religious communities, and society in general. Reclaiming our true self awareness with the support of a trustworthy group, even a small one, is especially strengthening and can improve our relationship with the world.

A special healing takes place when we regain in a group
that which we once lost in a group.

Being genuinely supported and celebrated by a group as you open to your true self can repattern your personality to feel that now the world welcomes you and that there really is a place for you—the *true* you—in the world after all. That in itself can be a breakthrough to greater freedom, safety, and belonging. It might be just what you need to stop holding yourself back—and to move full steam ahead into a life of purpose and passion.

When your group discusses the chapters that tell my story, I suggest reflecting on the ways *you* have experienced inner guidance, or times your connection with true self has opened new doors and led you into enriching territory you hadn't expected. You might not be giving yourself enough credit for those experiences, or you may have forgotten some of them. I found that as I wrote those chapters, my appreciation for myself and my life expanded. As you look at your life that way, the same can happen for you.

This book is for you. As you read it, may you experience a deep sense of peace and well-being that is your true self.

With love,
Martia Nelson*

*Martia is pronounced like Marsha.

Part I

MY STORY

I Begin the Return

1
Opening

In 1984 I heard a voice that changed my life. It was my voice, but it came from a place deep within me that I had never known existed. It told me I was going to have to change my workaholic lifestyle or I was going to die.

I was 34 years old and had spent the last seven years immersed in a successful career I loved. I was co-owner and director of a personal growth center—as well as an instructor of the acupressure and therapeutic massage curriculum taught there to students in professional training. My unusual work combination allowed me to express a full range of my personality: my business competitiveness, my creativity, and my ability to communicate with people at a deeply nurturing level.

I loved my work, but I had become addicted to it with an intensity I could not control. I worked evenings and weekends, and when I wasn't working, I was thinking about work. I could no longer relax on vacations so I stopped taking them. When friends called to suggest getting together, my first reaction was irritation that they wanted to intrude on my work time.

I rarely was sick, but I rarely felt well either. I should have noticed that the work I had devoted my life to was now draining the life out of me. But I kept going, until the inner voice spoke and I was able to listen.

It happened in an acupressure session I was receiving from a woman, Aminah Raheem, who had been one of my teachers. Suffering from stress and exhaustion, I lay fully clothed on Aminah's massage table as she gently held a series of acupressure points on my body to help me relax. Half an hour into the session I felt a discomfort, like anxiety, in my belly. Aminah put a reassuring hand on my belly and said, "What is your belly saying to you?"

I was about to say, "I don't know," but to my surprise I *did* know my belly's message. It was clear and definite as I spoke it out loud: "If you do not stop all the work you are doing and learn a new way to live, you are going to die." It went on to explain, "You are ready for work that takes you to a deeper level of connecting with people. To find this work, you must stop what you are doing now. You are so depleted that if you do not stop, you will die within a year in an accident or in 20 years from cancer."

As this revelation emerged I had two distinctly different, but simultaneous, reactions. On one level I was shocked. I started sobbing and wailing as my body felt the impact of the message. Facing the reality of death, my body was filled with fear and grief more powerful than anything I had ever felt before.

Yet, at the same time, there was a place deep within me that was completely calm and well, untouched by any of the emotion. At that level there was no worry, no fear, no disturbance whatsoever. It was a core of grace and peace beyond all distress I might feel. I realized the message was coming from this inner core and everything it was saying was true.

Then the message concluded: "Very few people have the opportunity to witness the beginning of their death. You have a choice to make about whether this is yours."

I didn't know it at the time, but this was my first experience of both my personality and true self. By feeling the distress of my personality while accepting true self's greater state of unwavering peace and well-being, I was able to make what was perhaps, up to that point, the most important and well-informed decision of my life. After letting that session reverberate within me for a couple weeks, I quit my work.

That decision was a huge leap into the unknown. I had no idea what my new work would be, so I lived in free-fall for more than a year. During that time, I often felt insecure and afraid as a result of letting go of my "old" life. In giving up my work I relinquished an identity I had clung to for almost decade. Each month I had no idea how I would get the money to live. I was without a love relationship to give me continuity or comfort. And while I needed support more than ever, I let old friendships drop, feeling they no longer "fit." It was as though everything that had been real to me before—or, more accurately, had made me real to myself—had become too vaporous to hold onto anymore.

With my external world in such change, I began looking within— into the thoughts, feelings, and beliefs that had been driving me all my life. The details of this inner landscape were fuzzy at first, but I felt pulled to keep looking. Before long, old pain surfaced as my most distressing childhood experiences presented themselves to me, desperate for release. My mother had been an alcoholic who could turn from genuinely loving and supportive to verbally vindictive in an instant. My father had been a rageaholic who yelled and shoved me around the family room several times a year, often pinning me to the wall or the floor.

As I relived memories of the physical abuse and emotional isolation, I was flooded with old feelings of fear, shame, and helplessness. For weeks at a time, an unrelenting ache in my chest reminded me that I still felt unlovable and alone. With the help of skilled body/mind therapists, and through lonely hours of my own inner processing, I slowly came to terms with what was happening. All inner injury that had kept me from having a more fulfilling life was now demanding my attention so it could be healed. This process was painful, frightening, and time-consuming, yet it was one of the most significant periods of my life.

In the midst of my soul-searching, a friend told me about a woman named Linda who did "intuitive readings," in which she communicated information from her higher guidance to help people in their spiritual growth. In the hope of getting greater perspective on what I was going through, I made an appointment for a reading.

Linda's technique was simple. She closed her eyes, went into a light meditation, and asked for higher guidance, inviting a greater perspective based in love and wisdom to come through her. The session was fascinating, and the information I received from her made me feel recognized at a deep level. From her greater perspective, Linda described aspects of my spirit that I had sensed but had never been able to put into clear thoughts or words. Toward the end of the session she told me that I, too, could receive higher guidance directly, if I chose to. She suggested sitting for ten minutes, three times a day, with the intention of quietly listening.

The suggestion that I could directly receive information from a higher source surprised me. I had assumed very few people could do this, only those who were gifted and somehow chosen for this special work, so I had never thought of trying it. Now being told I could have contact with a source of expanded knowledge and unconditional love stirred a longing in me that I had never let myself feel. I had lived much of my life with a buried grief, a sense that I had lost something deep within. It had to do with a vague memory of spiritual family, a family that extended beyond the people I knew and even beyond the physical realm. I felt that somewhere in this greater connectedness was my true source, and I longed to find it. My grief at feeling separated from it went beyond emotion; it was a spiritual yearning for Home.

After a few weeks of sitting and listening within as Linda had suggested, I was getting nowhere. I felt frustrated and disappointed. Why did she tell me I could do this if I couldn't? I phoned her and complained. She listened patiently, and then checked in with her guidance. "You're not ready," she reported back.

I hit the ceiling. "If I'm not ready, why did you get my hopes up? Why did you tell me I could do something I can't do?" I wanted to experience the contact so much.

"It's not that you can't do it. You're just not quite ready because there is something you're blocking," Linda said gently.

I started to say, "I'm not blocking anything!" but before I could get the words out, tears streamed down my face, and a new clarity emerged. "Oh, I know, it's that I'm going to have to move," I told Linda. "If I really listen, it's clear that my deeper self needs me to move out of the area. I'll leave this house that I've lived in for so long and loved so much. Home is so important to me. It's the hardest thing for me to leave." The barrier was broken.

2

Truth

Often in our daily lives we block things we don't want to hear because of the conflict we'll feel. Yet in turning to higher guidance we ask for the truth. To the degree we want to expand beyond our previous limitations, we long for truth. But to the degree we still want control over the details of our lives, we resist the truth and fear its touch. The pull toward truth is often equaled by our resistance to it. This ambivalence is our reluctance to choose between empowerment and control.

When truth touches us, every structure in our lives that was built on nontruth is destined for change. When I let in the truth about needing to move away, I finally allowed truth to touch me. My house was my last holdout, the last tangible symbol of my old self I still clung to. In finally loosening my grasp on the house, I recognized that the inner power guiding me was beyond my control, and its being beyond my control *was the very reason* it could propel me forward. I knew then that my safety was in my trust of this powerful source, not in my efforts to control it.

I also realized that higher guidance doesn't "impose" an agenda but simply offers information and options that support our highest good. Listening to our inner source of higher guidance (true self) and following its suggestions never require that we surrender our free will or override our better judgment. Rather, when we use it properly, higher guidance helps us open to our deepest, most empowering truth and integrate it into our daily living. Our challenge is to give up our tendency to deny our inner truth; only then are we really free to follow it.

3
Personality and True Self

For the first year my contact with higher guidance was like tender young shoots of new growth. I felt vulnerable and protective, sharing what was happening with very few people. I was afraid I wouldn't be believed or that old friends would judge me as unworthy of such a precious experience.

I took time every day to close my eyes and sit quietly, asking for assistance in every aspect of my life. In response an expanded, inner panorama of awareness opened to me. I was given a deeper view of each situation, one that was loving and revealed a purpose greater than I had been able to see with my ordinary perception. Higher guidance, or true self, spoke to me with more compassion and kindness than I had ever given myself—or than anyone else had ever given me.

My personality was being re-parented by my true self with the unconditional love and unwavering compassion I had missed as a child. I was being taught to see myself, others, and the world through that expanded perspective. As a result I began to have greater self-compassion than ever, to see my life more clearly, and to feel less afraid and alone.

To my surprise, true self kept showing me that nothing about my life was really wrong! This was difficult for me to comprehend because my life seemed so obviously topsy-turvy, and my mind frequently told me I was doomed. Yet true self patiently showed me the divinity, love, and hidden order in every situation, introducing me time and time again to the deeper perspective. My heart recognized this truth, and I began to learn.

One of the most helpful lessons was that we live in split realities: personality and true self. Most people call personality the *ego*. Personality is our conscious self, conditioned to see the world through the eyes of limitation, to judge ourselves and others, and to keep tight rules about what we can and cannot do in life. Personality sees a small reality, not the greater reality that cradles it.

True self, on the other hand, patiently stands by, offering the unwavering knowledge that a state of vibrant well-being and unlimited possibility is our true nature, a birthright that can be lived if we choose to do so. True self is our unlimited spirit; it sees beyond the personality's blinders into an unlimited reality that is the essence of creation and in which all things are possible.

The term *true self* is not meant to imply that any part of who we are is false or unreal. All aspects of our being are real to us at the level at which we perceive them, and they all have value. True self refers to the *essence* of our being that perceives all and is all. True self is completely aware of its expanded nature no matter what may be happening in our lives, and no matter what our personality is thinking, feeling, or doing.

> *True self is undiminished by the personality's suffering*
> *and always sees the bigger picture.*

As I became more aware of my true self, I sensed when I was drawing awareness from that source and when I was not. I realized that my true self had been within me all my life, quietly guiding me along, yet I had not identified with it. My identity had been with my personality. The feelings, beliefs, and expectations of my personality had been my yardstick for measuring my success, safety, sanity, and personal well-being. The problem had been that my personality could only see the smaller picture and had operated entirely from conditioning and past experience.

Now I was in a bind. My personality told me to tighten control of my life. It was panicked by the new things I was doing. Yet my true self rejoiced in my growth, showing me that I had changed the direction of my life at every level as an entry into something greater.

Often my personality invalidated the information I received through my true's self guidance, and I was challenged to choose which source to believe. So for months I lived with *both* realities and their apparently conflicting information. Magically, everything true self told me ultimately turned out to be true, even against seemingly impossible odds. And in spite of my personality's repeated warnings, I did not go broke, did not die, and did not end up crazy or alone. Instead, something within me shifted to incorporate true self into my identity, and I learned a new way to live.

4

My Search

The turning point came through a rite of passage tailor-made for me. Because it was my area of greatest resistance—my personality's last stand—the drama unfolded around leaving my house. After I realized I needed to move, I packed most of my belongings and tried to figure out where I would be going. I sensed that a new home was waiting for me, but I couldn't quite sense where. My true self told me that tracking my new home would strengthen me and teach me a new way of living.

After I had agonized over my dilemma for a few months, the name of a specific town popped into my mind, out of the blue, during a light meditation. I set off for that area a few days later and when I arrived, I knew it was home. Finding the right house was easy; the third one I looked at was definitely mine. I made an offer right away and couldn't wait to move in.

Everything was perfect. My offer was accepted. The bank said there would be no problem with my loan. I put my old house on the market and was confident it would sell quickly. In a few short weeks I would leave the crowded city and settle in the country where everything was green. Cows would live across the street from me! I was delighted with where my intuition was taking me at last.

Then the trouble started. The bank called and told me they had made a mistake and could not possibly approve my loan. Round and round we went; they wouldn't budge. On top of that, my house wasn't selling, though at that time it was a seller's market and less attractive houses nearby sold within days.

As the deadline for buying my new house approached, things looked grim. People began to tell me the situation was impossible. Banks told me. The realtor trying to sell my old house told me. Even the realtor representing me in buying the new house told me. Well-meaning friends tried to prepare me for the disappointment they saw coming. That was when I learned to hate the often-heard "spiritual" axiom: "When you're doing what's really right, everything happens easily and effortlessly." (I'm here to say now that that is not always true!)

I was torn inside. For the first time in my life I had clearly heard the intuitive voice of my true self, recognized it as real, and followed it by taking major action based on its guidance. I had chosen the expansive reality of true self over the restrictive reality of my personality. I had made the shift.

The planned move to my house felt so deeply right, more right than anything had ever felt. Yet outer events clearly contradicted that inner certainty. My confidence was shaken. Was I fooling myself about true self guidance being real? Did this mean I could never really trust myself again?

At my wit's end, I consulted true self. Peace and clarity flowed through me instantly: "Of course that's your new house. You found your home, and you will live there. Do not give up on yourself. What appears to be most real often isn't. Everything will work out."

The third time my realtor called to tell me we should admit defeat and cancel my offer on the new house, I was clear. I said, "My higher guidance has told me that it's all going to work, and I have confidence in that." Who knows what she thought, but she didn't argue anymore.

Finally we found a way to satisfy the bank's concerns, and my loan got last-minute approval. At eight o'clock on the night before the deadline, someone bought my old house. Everything happened smoothly and quickly from then on, and I soon moved into my new home. With that move came my first tangible step into the new territory that had beckoned me for so long. I had crossed over, and with at least one foot firmly planted on new ground, my journey Home had truly begun.

5

The Overview

Why had my transition been so difficult? I had been going through a move into new consciousness. Because part of my transition had included the experience of living in split realities, I had manifested the clarity of my true self (through my intuition, or inner guidance) as well as the resistance within my personality (through the outer obstacles with the house). To the degree I opened to true self, I found my way. And to the degree I allowed the limitations of my personality's old beliefs and fears to restrict me, my outer way was obstructed.

The dynamics had been simple, though only hindsight allowed me to see it that way. While lost in the drama I had been blind much of the time, feeling my way moment to moment but unable to see the bigger picture. Yet that had been the challenge, the true test. Those moments of choosing greater truth and acting on it had strengthened my alignment with true self and had kept me on my path.

6
Seeing

After I had made the move to my new house, my reality expanded in leaps and bounds. Helping other people rediscover their true self became my new work. Through the process of guiding them, I witnessed and learned profound truths about life and the unlimited being we all are. Seeing myself and others with this new sight opened worlds of possibilities to me. The chapters ahead hold my favorites of those early, but timeless, insights.

Those insights began coming in 1985 when I started offering sessions to clients. In these sessions, people asked about their greatest personal issues: happiness, purpose, work, relationships, and so on. They wanted a bigger picture that illuminated the spiritual dynamics underlying their struggles and provided a more loving, compassionate perspective for viewing themselves. They longed to feel seen and celebrated for who they truly were. My job was to look with a deeper seeing, as Linda had done for me, and help them experience their true self in ways that would enrich and expand their lives. Doing that became one of my greatest joys.

My original technique was simple: Take a few moments to drop into a meditative state and open my awareness to true self. As I did that, an expanded perspective of spiritual information I had never known or perceived before presented itself. For an hour or more I received that information and spoke it to the person—and simultaneously felt the profound wisdom and beauty of it absorbed into my body and my personality, becoming part of me at every level in a full imprint throughout my being. For the entire session, I was bathed in a flow of unwavering love and well-being, which I came to recognize as our most natural, essential nature—our true self state. This flow of expanded information and loving well-being taught me as much as it taught my clients.

I called this technique *true self channeling* because I was opening myself as a clear channel to true self's expanded perspective. Relating to people through *true self channeling* was new territory for me. At last I understood the "deeper way of connecting with people" foretold to me on Aminah's massage table. Classes and speaking engagements quickly followed, and I found that I kept getting this deep, spiritual education no matter when or where I channeled true self.

Because the nature of my work was so dynamic and alive, it kept evolving over the years. I learned and grew with it. Now, after more than two decades, I have acquired a wide range of techniques in addition to true self channeling, so I refer to my sessions with the umbrella term *coaching* or *mentoring*. *Life and business coaching* and *true self mentoring* are two terms I currently use, but they may change as my work keeps evolving.

I love all that I do. Yet the true self channeling continues to be the technique that reveals new information consistently richer, deeper, and more helpful than anything I could have thought of in my personality's ordinary state of awareness—while providing the "missing piece" needed by the client I am addressing.

For example, one woman came to me saying, "I'm stuck. I'm not moving forward in my life like I should. I hate my job, and for months I've been pushing myself to look for a new one, but I'm not following through. Every time I think of job hunting, I immediately lose energy and do nothing. I'm dragging my feet in other areas, too. What's wrong with me that I'm so stuck?"

I closed my eyes and opened to true self. An inner panorama instantly appeared, showing that this woman was not stuck at all: She was waiting. In the image, she stood with her toes touching, but not crossing, a line dividing her life into two territories, the one she was leaving and the one she was about to enter. She wasn't moving forward yet because she was waiting to complete an internal shift that would help her to succeed in her new territory.

In the territory she was leaving, her focus had been surviving: struggling hard but just getting by, being overwhelmed by crises, feeling she didn't deserve much, and always having a schedule so demanding that it depleted her. In the territory she was about to enter, her new focus would be thriving: daily feeling ease, happiness, compassion, abundance, creativity, safety, peace, and the flow of life's goodness through her.

While transitioning from the struggle and suffering of survival based living to the vibrant well-being of thrival based living, she was pausing to give her personality time to develop a stronger taproot into true self. She needed to acclimate to true self well-being as her new, driving force—and her personality needed to develop new energy circuits to carry it. True self well-being was to become her new fuel, propelling her into her new territory and then guiding and sustaining her. Rushing forward too soon, before her personality had become rooted in that well-being, would have caused her to run out of fuel. Although her personality hadn't been able to see it, her deeper wisdom had been making her wait.

Her inner shift would also elicit changes in her thinking and self-perception, which needed to be less oriented to the struggle and suffering of survival and more oriented to the vibrant well-being of thrival. "I'm changing jobs because I hate my old job" would become "I'm changing jobs because I choose fulfilling work in a supportive environment." "I don't deserve ease. I feel more at home with struggle" would become "I enjoy and deserve ease. I'm drawn to it." "Life is hard, and I feel stuck" would become "I like feeling in the flow of life." "I please or impress others to gain well-being" would become "I open to the true self well-being always present within me."

I channeled this information, and more, to the woman for an hour. It rang true to her, and helped her to trust and appreciate herself. We talked another half hour about how she would apply the information. She left the session with new self-confidence, clarity, well-being, and practical tools to help her thrive. She was ready to deeply support and care for herself.

True self channeling is a joyous experience for me. I feel the most balanced while channeling than at any other time or in any other activity. True self channeling not only helps me to reveal new, expanded perspectives to clients and students, it remains *my* primary source of spiritual education. I learn new things every time I channel, regardless of whether the channeling is for others or myself.

During the entire period I'm channeling, the pure love and well-being of true self stream through me, bathing me within. Unity, our Oneness with everyone and everything—our *being* one source—is real to me and seems the most natural perception in the world. And as information comes through me in words, I *experience* it as though it is imprinting directly into my body and expanding my personality's perception of reality.

True self channeling also keeps showing me that our personality is not who we are; we are always more. I am given this lesson whenever a client's personality clashes with mine (yes, this happens!). One man got on my nerves in the first two minutes by criticizing things in my office before he had even sat down. Then he wanted a very specific focus to his session but wouldn't quite tell me what it was. I felt him block me at every turn.

Exasperated, I considered referring him to someone else. Instead, I followed an intuitive feeling to go ahead with the session. As soon as I opened to true self channeling, everything shifted. My perspective deepened, and I no longer saw a difficult person. I saw this man suffering from the deep pain of having lost touch with the amazing beauty and love he carried within. It felt natural then to address him with love and honor, relating to him as he truly was rather than as his personality presented him.

Conscious, true self experience is not so integrated into my personality that I'm in it continuously throughout my day, but it's available when I remember to choose it, and I increasingly see its positive effects in my life. Its most precious gift to me has been the lesson that we are all more than we appear to be.

7

Sounding

A year into working with clients, something surprising suddenly happened. As I turned inward to channel true self, I started feeling an impulse to open my mouth and make nonverbal sounds. What the sounds would be I had no idea, but the impulse was strong and persistent. I resisted a few times, not wanting to appear foolish or weird to my clients, and then asked true self about it when I was alone.

"Go with it, and trust it. Make the sounds, even if for only a few seconds, and explain to your clients that you're just trying something new," was the message I received. "Follow the sounds. They're taking you somewhere."

So I did what true self suggested. I felt awkward and embarrassed as I did my few seconds of sounding for clients before the verbal channeling. People were receptive, and no one seemed to be judging me but me. With time I gained confidence and allowed the sounding to continue longer, up to five minutes or more.

To better understand what was happening, I also sounded for myself when I was alone. It was then I began to love the sound and to experience the world it was opening to me. Through my sounding I realized that everything, *everything*, in our world is sound. Again, *everything is sound.*

We humans are such visual creatures that most of us can go our whole lives defining physical reality predominantly by what we see. "Seeing is believing." Audible reality seems second to visual reality: *We unconsciously believe there is less to hear in the world than to see.* I was beginning to perceive differently.

As I sounded, I perceived that not only is everyone and everything made of sound, but that sound surrounds us. I don't mean that everyone and everything creates sound; I mean that everyone and everything *is* sound and emanates the sound that it *is.*

Everyone and everything emanates its sound all the time, everywhere!

Every blade of grass, tree, cloud, rock, flower, and cell in our bodies— as well as every inanimate object in the world—is sound and emanates the sound it is. The vast majority of those sounds are outside the vibrational range we consciously hear, so we move through the world unaware that they are as present around us as air. Over the millennia, our ears and brains have evolved to register only the miniscule range of sounds directly related to our physical survival.

In my sounding sessions, I closed my eyes, turned my awareness inward to true self, opened my mouth, and let sounds come through me—much the way I received words in true self channeling. Surrendered to an intuitive and creative process, I wasn't consciously controlling or directing the sounds. Impulses to sound in specific ways gently guided me, and I followed them as best I could. I called the sounds *true self sounds*.

They came in spontaneous, unpredictable sequences that were not consistent enough to be called chanting. They also lacked the melody or organization of song. I saw no logical patterns. In fact, while I was making one sound, I had no idea how long it would last, what the next one would be, or where they all were leading. So I stayed in the moment and allowed the orchestration to unfold in its own mysterious way.

The range of sounds varied greatly: high, low, soft and quiet, strong and loud, lovely, enticing, rough, unpolished, odd, and more. Sometimes they were rhythmic, sometimes not. I liked some but not others; most were sounds I was not used to making. Often they seemed ancient, like sounds lost to us over the ages that still linger as vibrational memories, ready to be reactivated the instant we open to them. "This was our original language before words or intellect developed" was a phrase that came to me frequently.

Even more profound to me than the way the sounds sounded was the way they felt. All of them, even the softest and quietest, even the ones I thought didn't sound "good", created vibrations that felt purposeful and pleasurable as they moved through me. My body felt like a musical instrument being played by true self.

The bones in the right side of my face might vibrate with one sound, and then my skull might vibrate with the next one. Then it might be both sides of my face, or the back of my throat, or my chest, or my belly, or my left hip. I never knew which part of my body would be "played" next because I never knew what the next sound would be, but it all felt glorious.

As in all my work, no one else was controlling me or the sounds. My personality simply was relinquishing direction to a deeper aspect of my own being—true self, of course. I could have stopped or changed the sounding at any point, much the way we can stop or change a spontaneous song, poem, or painting we're creating. Yet, as often is the case with such creative processes, the sounding worked best when I let it come through without interfering. In a state of surrender to a deep expressiveness, my personality kept its hands off the steering wheel as much as possible and went along for the marvelous ride.

My personal sounding sessions began lasting longer, usually 10 to 20 minutes but sometimes 45 minutes to an hour. They always left me feeling enlivened, balanced, and nourished. Expansive information presented itself internally as I sounded, much as it did during verbal channeling. Usually it gave me a bigger picture for a personal issue I was facing, but occasionally I experienced vignettes from other lifetimes, usually long ago. Whether they were my lifetimes or other people's I can't say for sure. They felt real to me as I sounded, complete with emotion, visual images, and spiritual perspective. They always increased my understanding of my life and of life in general, so I was deeply grateful.

By sounding I discovered that nonverbal sound can carry far more information than verbal language. In verbal language, information is presented linearly, one word after the other, and it takes time to speak, write, read, or listen to all those words. True self sound, however, is not linear. It is multidimensional and outside time: A lot happens, and it happens all at once. True self sound is jam-packed with multiple levels of information, all communicated simultaneously and instantly.

For example, if we have five concepts to communicate verbally, we speak or write them one at a time; and to communicate effectively, we organize them into a sequence in which each concept leads logically to the next. But those same five concepts communicated through true self sound are presented all at once in a cluster. Even richer than that, *the emotional, visceral, visual (mental images), intellectual, and spiritual experiences of all five concepts are presented simultaneously, in seconds.* Or in a split second. This complex information is transmitted as a whole. Information "sounded" in a minute might take 30 minutes or an hour to speak—and still the spoken version would lack the depth of experiential imprint that comes with true self sound.

One day while watching a TV program on PBS about whales, I was surprised and delighted to hear this aspect of my sounding experience apparently confirmed by science. "We now can measure the amount of information communicated in whale songs," I remember the researcher saying. "We can't decipher the content yet, so we can't tell *what* whales are saying to each other, but we can tell *how much* they are saying. A 30-minute whale song conveys approximately as much information as Homer's *The Iliad*."

In addition to using true self sound to gain expansive information and awareness, I sound for the most practical reasons. Sounding tethers me to true self's unwavering well-being no matter where I am. When I'm stuck in traffic, tense and anxious because I left home late and now am getting even later by the minute, doing just three breaths of true self sounds as I drive instantly soothes and calms me. Or in the morning, doing true self sound for the brief time it takes to put on my slippers and robe is enough to create inner balance and harmony that affects me the whole day.

One client I taught to do true self sounding got creative using it. A self-described "extremely analytical person" prone to multi-tasking her way through her day, she had been uncomfortable meditating because she couldn't quiet her mind. Then she started doing true self sounding as a preamble to meditating—sounding for a few minutes first—and her mind became quiet and peaceful in meditation. She also found that during periods of increased stress in her life, sounding for even just two minutes a day made her life noticeably more peaceful and enjoyable.

Sounding helped her with problem solving, too. As a small business owner, she sometimes faced difficult employee issues or sales challenges. When she felt stuck, she would hold the problem in her mind for a moment; then she would release it and sound for five to ten minutes. "The sounding makes me feel calm and open to new ideas," she told me. "Within a day, an answer always comes to me that I never would have figured out in my usual, analytical approach."

Perhaps the reason true self sounding is so potent, and assists us in ways ranging from the most expansive to the most practical, is that it energetically integrates the vibrations of true self's unlimitedness into the personality's limited consciousness. The sound comes from a deeper level than our beliefs or emotions and imprints the boundless knowing, unconditional love, and unwavering well-being of true self into the personality's reality.

8
Your True Self Channeling and Sounding

If it appeals to you, I invite you to tune into your true self's loving guidance in your own way. It may be sitting quietly and listening for that inner, intuitive voice—and then speaking it out loud or writing its messages in your journal. Or it may be through creative expression such as dancing, painting, singing, or playing a musical instrument.

At the end of this chapter, there are meditations to help you get started. As with all suggestions in this book, use them in whatever way is most empowering and balancing for you, and feel free to make changes if other words or formats work better for you. There are two constants, however: True self's guidance *always* comes with love and empowerment, and it *never* overrides your own choices and common sense.

If you receive information that scares you, criticizes you, makes you feel bad about yourself or your life, disempowers you in any way, or conveys ill feelings about other people or the world—or if it pressures you to take specific action—it is NOT coming from true self. The personality thinks that way, but true self does not. If that happens, recognize that your personality has been activated and is trying to help, but that its perspective is too limited to be truly helpful.

Do not reject your personality any more than you would reject a two-year-old child for telling you how to drive a car. Imagine that you help your personality into a special child's seat in the back seat, where it can ride as a cherished passenger and look out the window while your true self drives. Then, remember that true self is deeper, wiser, and more loving than the personality, and invite your true self to guide you. True self sees everyone and everything with love, compassion, and appreciation. *All* of true self's guidance will increase your well-being, not diminish it.

People who do these meditations often want to start getting "good" information right away and become disappointed or frustrated if this doesn't happen. Think of this process as turning on a faucet that has been shut off for years. At first the water might be rusty, not ready for drinking, but after it has run for some time it gets clear. Similarly, as you open to true self guidance, the flow through your newly opened channel might be "rusty" for quite a while. Information may not make sense, or it may carry your personality's judgment—or it may be clear, loving true self guidance that you simply do not know how to use yet.

Be content to let the guidance run through you, without doing anything with it, for as long as it takes to become clear, supportive, and usable for you. And even if you never actually *do* anything with the guidance, that is fine. You will be sitting in the flow of love, compassion, and well-being while channeling; that is the most important part. That love will be imprinting into your personality's consciousness and into the cells and tissues in your body, and at some point it will emanate into your life to create greater love, compassion, and well-being for you there.

If you do not think you are getting any actual information, do not worry. One of two things is probably happening: 1.) Your conscious awareness is not yet attuned to the subtlety of true self's communication. Continuing to practice over time will likely attune your awareness so that, at some point, you will become conscious of the information. 2.) Your style of receiving guidance is nonverbal, in which case it is natural that you are not conscious of verbal content. The loving, true self information still imprints within you, teaching your personality and emanating into your life. In either case, the most important thing is to enjoy the subtle flow of well-being through you while you are channeling or sounding. (I recommend that you *not* take important action or make major changes in your life based solely on your true self channeling.)

As with everything in this book, if either of these meditations does not feel right for you, is not pleasant, or actually distresses you, stop doing it and move into an activity that balances and nourishes you. If you need to talk about your experience with someone, get that support. Stay with exercises that increase your well-being and let go of ones that don't.

MEDITATION
TRUE SELF CHANNELING

1. Sit quietly and notice your breathing. Every breath is a good breath, no matter how deep or shallow, and breathes life-sustaining oxygen into your body. . . .

2. Assume that each breath is automatically breathing you a little deeper into true self. Even if you are not sure exactly what or where your true self is, imagine that your breath has innate intelligence that *does* know. Each breath gently breathes you a little deeper into true self. . . .

3. Think or say a phrase like, "I open to true self's love and guidance, for the highest good."

4. Ask a question or imagine you are handing true self an issue you want guidance about. If you can't think of a question or specific issue, simply make a general request such as, "What is the most helpful information for me right now?"

5. Assume that each breath gently continues to breathe you a little deeper into true self. . . .

6. As any information comes to you, speak it out loud or write it down. Or if you choose another creative medium—such as dancing, painting, or making music—begin that activity, and assume that true self's information is flowing through you as you do it. If you do not notice any information, do not worry; just assume that it is too subtle for you to notice yet, and that it is supporting and guiding you at a subconscious level. . . .

7. When you are ready to bring your true self channeling to a close, sit or lie down and relax for a few minutes. Then stretch and look around, and slowly transition to the next activity in your day.

MEDITATION
TRUE SELF SOUNDING

1. Sit quietly and notice your breathing. Every breath is a good breath, no matter how deep or shallow, and breathes life-sustaining oxygen into your body. . . .

2. Assume that each breath is automatically breathing you a little deeper into true self. Even if you are not sure exactly what or where your true self is, imagine that your breath has innate intelligence that *does* know. Each breath gently breathes you a little deeper into true self. . . .

3. Think or say a phrase like, "I open to the sound of true self's love and guidance, for the highest good."

4. Open your mouth and let sounds come out. If no sound offers itself, start playing with sounds. Assume that every sound is the right sound, and that true self's energy is automatically in every sound you make. Look for the gentle pleasure in each sound. . . .

5. When you are ready to bring your true self sounding to a close, sit or lie down and relax for a few minutes. Then stretch and look around, and slowly transition to the next activity in your day.

NOTE: The purpose of these meditations is experiential only and is not meant to replace your own good judgment about choices and actions you take in your life. If information you receive empowers and balances you, and if you feel the ring of truth in it, then it may be information *to consider*. The fact that you received it does not mean that it is "right" or that you need to do anything differently in your life. It is okay to receive information and do nothing with it, especially in the learning stage.

Part II

INNER GUIDANCE

Listening to Spirit Within

9

Higher Guidance or Inner Guidance?

You have just read the story of my most life-changing event: opening to and learning from the intuitive guidance of true self. It transformed a lifestyle that was depleting me and heading me toward a health crisis to one that nourished me and led me into rich, new territory I had never dreamed possible—but for which, deep down, I had had silent, unconscious longings.

For the first decade or more, I kept thinking and speaking of this source of guidance as *higher guidance*. And, in fact, the title of this chapter in previous editions was *Higher Guidance*. It is time that I update that term.

At first, Spirit or spiritual guidance seemed separate from me so I called it *higher guidance* and referred to my channeling as *channeling higher guidance*. The word *higher* implied that the consciousness I was drawing from was above me on a hierarchy of consciousness, greater than anything I could access within myself. The thought that I might be receiving information from "just myself" horrified me! I still identified myself as my personality, which indeed would have been a limited source from which to draw.

Yet as I continued opening to higher guidance over the years, the dividing line I thought existed between it and myself faded. At one point I realized that my true self had been on the "council" of higher guidance all along. Then I began seeing that the true self of everyone I had been coaching and doing true self channeling for was also on that council. From there I recognized that the true self of everyone on our planet was part of higher guidance.

In time, I saw that divine realms and expansive states of being beyond our earthly awareness informed higher guidance as well. Although words become inadequate past this point, and most of it is still beyond my conscious understanding, I could tell that the medium of communication among all contributing realms, beings, and states of being was Unity, the very state toward which our own conscious awareness is evolving.

Over the following few years I saw that we all had access to this unlimited spiritual guidance through our true self, so I drifted away from the term *higher guidance* and started saying *inner guidance* and *channeling inner guidance*, or *true self guidance* and *channeling true self*. I saw true self as our personal doorway to universal source.

As more time passed, I realized that everyone's true self is so expansive and unlimited that it blends into everyone else's true self, without any separation or individuation. In that image, true self was not a doorway to universal source; it was universal source itself.

I saw true self as one shared beingness
of unlimited intelligence, love, and creativity.

This perception grew as I worked with clients. When I looked at someone from simply my personality, I saw their body and personality. As I opened my awareness to my true self, I perceived their true self. As I looked deeper, I saw that our two true selves merged into one. Continuing deeper, our shared true self merged with the true selves of others, and we *all* shared the same true self. Deeper still, true self became a state of unlimited, creative intelligence from which everyone and everything is made. I saw it as our essence, individually and collectively. It was the source of creation *and* the creative material itself. True self knew everything because it *was* everything, including us.

Another way to imagine this is with the metaphor of an inverted funnel. The top is small and represents our personality's limited awareness while the bottom fans out, representing our true self's expansive awareness. If we start at the top and slowly move down the center of the funnel, our awareness expands as the funnel does.

When we arrive at the depth where the bottom of the funnel should be, we notice that the funnel doesn't end, it simply keeps expanding so far that it blends with the funnels of people around us. Our true selves blend into one.

Still we keep dropping deeper, and soon we are below the place where all the funnels blend. We are in spaciousness that no longer has any individual boundaries or identity. There is one open, expansive, unlimited true self for all of us: one source of boundless intelligence and creativity.

As we go deeper still, we see that true self is Source. It is the beingness that creates and sustains all things and all beings. We are made of this beingness. As the creator and sustainer of all things and all beings, there is nothing that true self does not know and cannot do.

True self is not just an aspect of who we are.
It is the totality of our being, and of ALL being.

To some people this is a description of God or Spirit. Perhaps you choose to call it Source, the Universe, the Beloved, Light, or another term that opens your heart and reminds you that you are a cherished part of the magnificent scheme of life. Please feel free to adjust my terms to be in harmony with yours.

10
How Accessible is Inner Guidance?

I believe we all draw on inner guidance (or true self) continuously, just as we draw on the life-giving oxygen in air with each breath we take. And just as most of our breaths are taken unconsciously, most of our communication with inner guidance is automatic and goes unnoticed. Yet, in spite of our lack of conscious awareness, the air we breathe is still real to our lungs and the guidance we receive is still real to our intuition. We are never truly alone, and somewhere deep within, we know this.

We can easily become more aware of the inner guidance we draw from so regularly. There are countless techniques and approaches to choose from, and many will be offered in this book. Any experience of opening to true self will lead us there. True self is the entrance into the greater realm. Through true self we open to unlimited being and allow unlimited experience to enter our lives.

11
How Do Inner Guidance and Higher Guidance Relate?

As I've mentioned, I believed higher guidance was outside myself because I had to view it that way to begin trusting it—until I increasingly noticed an inner aspect of my own being that was an exact match of the "outer" higher guidance. Focusing on the external source awakened my awareness of the internal one. This blossoming of my inner guidance dissolved the separation I felt from external higher guidance, allowing me to see inner and outer guidance as one and the same, a continuum of awareness that is omnipresent.

Even after reading about my transition, many people will relate better to ideas of higher guidance or outer guidance. I do not perceive one concept to be better or worse. Yet, whenever we turn to a higher guidance we consider external, and we do it *because we do not experience or believe in the unlimited spirit of our own being*, we are missing something wonderful and healing within us.

Turning to a higher guidance we believe is external can help us get in touch with the inner guidance of true self—as it did for me. Using external guidance can help us reconnect with the aspect of ourselves that matches it—and then help us learn to use our internal source more consciously. Yet, repeatedly relying on external guidance *to replace* inner guidance might not be beneficial in the long run. It can create an imbalance in our lives, with the external guidance becoming one more addiction we use to avoid and mistrust ourselves.

Higher guidance of a pure nature will not give information that takes us further from ourselves. Instead, it will be unconditionally generous with information that leads us to self-love and natural empowerment. With this guidance, we can learn to face the world with "loving eyes" that see everyone and everything, including ourselves, with unconditional love and compassion. This loving sight opens us to an unwavering recognition of perfection. We can surrender to life and follow its flow no matter where it takes us, for both inner and outer realities become trustworthy when we can see with love everywhere.

12
Guidance and Its Form

Now that we have discussed specific terms for guidance, I will put them all aside for the rest of this chapter. To be as inclusive of everyone as possible I will use the general term *spiritual guidance*, to simply mean guidance we receive through spirit, whether we perceive it as inner, or outer, or omnipresent.

People report wide variations in the forms in which they experience their spiritual guidance. Pure spirit has no form of its own: it is beyond form and does not identify with it. Yet as human beings we live in a world of form. Our personality is so identified with it that everything must have some form before we recognize it as real and are able to talk about it. Language is based on form, as are most thoughts. Because we receive conscious awareness of spiritual guidance through the filter of our personality, we interpret the experience through our individual and collective needs for form.

For example, if one person's personality feels more comfortable receiving spiritual guidance that comes in the image of a wizened old man in white robes with an ancient-sounding name, or as an angel, or as the spirit of nature, that is how they will experience it. If another person's unconscious need is for a group of spirits from a higher realm or an other-worldy feminine spirit, that is the form in which they will perceive their guidance. Or if yet another person needs to relate to a being who is very grounded with a strong personality, a sense of humor, and the ability to give factual data about events on earth, they may experience that. On the other hand, someone who is less attached to personal form may simply experience spiritual guidance as God (whatever God means to them), or radiant light, or as creative inspiration. The list of possible variations is limitless.

None of these forms is any better or worse than another; the form we give spiritual guidance doesn't necessarily matter. In fact, as we grow in consciousness, that form will very likely change to reflect our new perspectives.

To some people, an attachment to form might seem limiting, but it is simply a reality of our human consciousness. The personality's reality is based in form. We honor our need for spiritual growth by opening to spirit, and we honor our personality by doing it through form. Receiving spiritual guidance through form invites the personality to participate so it can be touched and transformed by the expansive experience. The refined frequency of spiritual guidance helps the personality expand its range of perceived reality and integrate greater awareness into daily life. It is, then, both wise and compassionate that we don't push aside our personality's needs as we open spiritually. And it is just as wise to remember that the spiritual source we open to is greater than anything our personality perceives.

Spiritual guidance is unconditionally loving and generous, willing to come to all of us in any way we allow it. It will never force its way through our personality's limitation, nor will it ever pass us up because we are not "evolved" enough to be worthy. Spiritual guidance honors us *as we are* and graciously works in harmony with both our limitations and our aspirations. Just keep in mind that the form guidance takes reflects more about the orientation of the person receiving it than about the spiritual source itself. What matters more than the form is the essence of the guidance, and the two should not be confused.

Because it is filtered through the beliefs and limitations of our personality, I believe all information we receive from spiritual guidance gets unintentionally distorted in some way. Although an individual may truly be tapping a pure spiritual source, the process of bringing that information into form is like translating information from an unlimited language into a limited one. Something always gets lost in the translation. The information is first filtered (at least slightly) by the beliefs, needs, and experiences of the individual. Then it is filtered again by the beliefs, needs, and experiences of each person who hears or reads the information.

Many people are spiritually clear and open, yet even the most aware human beings are still in bodies. Everyone functioning in a physical body has a personality, and even the most enlightened personality carries some filters. As we continue to evolve, honing our abilities to bring unlimited awareness through our personality, less distortion will appear. For the time being, simply be aware that no information credited to spiritual guidance conveys exactly and completely the truth that is intended.

How, then, can you know if information you read or hear from someone will benefit you? By fine tuning your own intuition and listening to it. Intuition is the voice of your true self. Your true self will always recognize truth and let you know whether information is relevant for you.

Someone else's expression of spiritual guidance is not meant to replace or invalidate your inner truth; it is meant to remind you of it. If you feel an inner reverberation of *Oh, yes, that rings true in me!* as you hear or read information from someone's spiritual guidance, follow that ring of truth *in yourself.* Let it take you to *your* inner source of truth and guidance.

No matter how much you trust or respect people (including me), do not believe anything just because they say it. The purpose of spiritual guidance, especially when it comes through other people, is to activate the source of greater knowing within *you* and make you more aware of it. *You* are your greatest guide.

Part III

SELF-LOVE

Your Source of Life

13

The Love That You Are

Vibrant love is in the bones, tissues, and physiology of your body. It is your essence, the seed energy for your emotions, thoughts, and awareness. No matter how complex, every element of your internal and external realities originates entirely from love. This love is the life force, the common denominator in all things and all beings. Through this life force you are one with everything and everyone in the world—and beyond.

Self-love is the experience of this love that you are. This love is a brilliant light. Like the sun or a star, it shines continuously in the core of your being, even when it is not seen or felt. When you have bouts of feeling unworthy, unlovable, resentful, or judgmental, the cloud cover of your personality has moved in and has blocked your experience of the light. But no matter what may prevent you from seeing or feeling the love that you are, the love is still there—always and unconditionally. As you learn self-love, you are simply learning to see through that cloud cover to the ever-shining light of your true self.

When you think about loving yourself, you may still be focused in the cloud cover. In trying to feel good about yourself, you may think, "I love myself because I am generous, sensitive, and have a loving heart. I care about people, and I am intelligent, and I really do look pretty good, and...." Cherishing those traits in your personality is valuable, but that is not truly self-love. Learning to appreciate certain patterns within the cloud cover is not the same as breaking through it.

What is beneath the cloud cover does not need to be loved—because it *is* love itself. Living with self-love is accepting the love that is your essence. You can allow the warmth of that light to shine through and be with you in your daily life—when you are alone, when you are quiet, even when you are in pain or under stress. Whether you feel joyous, loving, angry, or resentful does not matter. The love that you are is not dependent on how you feel or behave at the personality level. It is unconditional, meaning that it is there and available regardless of any conditions, including distressing emotions. Its light penetrates all aspects of your being, and you have it no matter how you feel.

You never have to "get over" any of
your feelings to find love.

If you are dealing with a painful feeling and cannot seem to move through it, you can still draw on the healing power of self-love. Perhaps you are lost in anger; you have a shield of defensiveness around you, and from behind it you are shaking your fists in pain and rage. Even in that intense anger, you can allow some of the warmth and vitality of the love that you are to seep through, to fill you alongside the frustration and hurt.

You do not have to give up your anger, sadness, despair, or other feelings. Allow the love that you are to shine through and touch you along with your feelings. Then you are empowering yourself: You are allowing your personality's emotion to be the vehicle for the unconditional love you are made of.

14
Loving Yourself and *Sweet Me*

One variation of self-love is self-compassion. It is your natural state, your birthright. Self-compassion is a gentle state because it is subtle and quiet, and it is a warrior's state because it is powerful for making life changes. To experience self-compassion, take a moment to close your eyes, and with each of your next three breaths, silently say the following words: *Sweet Me.* Then do it again, this time looking gently for the tiniest, most microscopic sensations of sweetness emanating through you. *Sweet Me.* Continue doing it for a few more breaths.

When saying *Sweet Me*, you are not trying to believe or feel that you are a sweet person—nothing could be more irrelevant, for that would occur in the personality's conditional beliefs or emotions. Rather, you are opening your awareness to the constant, unconditional sweetness that emanates through you always—but which you usually do not notice. That sweetness is always there because *it is the love you are made of.*

Self-compassion does not have loud bells and whistles or strong sensations. It is tiny and subtle. Microscopic. And it is the most powerful tool for transformation you might ever find. It is so powerful that it can work *even when you do not feel it* if you just keep opening to it anyway.

Self-compassion occurs whenever you open to the sweetness within you. When you are worried, close your eyes and let the words *Sweet Me* fall into you like leaves drifting to the ground. When you are sad, let *Sweet Me* settle alongside the sadness. When you are hurt, frightened or angry, let *Sweet Me* emanate through you while you feel that emotion. Intense emotion unbalances us—not because there is anything innately unbalancing in the emotion itself but because the emotion occurs in an environment void of self-compassion. Open to the tiniest sweetness within yourself as that emotion occurs, and you will notice a shift toward balance. You will begin to feel safer, calmer, and more alive.

Our spirit is made of love and compassion. Sweetness. When we open to self-compassion by saying *Sweet Me*, we open to Spirit, Source, God, true self. Self-compassion is the compassion of our spirit emanating within us. That compassion is unconditional; we don't have to do anything to deserve it or create it. Our only job is to let ourselves have it.

Without self-compassion we struggle, finding fault and rejecting ourselves in our efforts to become something better. That self-rejection hurts us and keeps us from thriving, intensifying our feeling of being separate from the goodness we seek. As we open to self-compassion, we automatically feel more acceptance of ourselves as we are. We can still choose to make changes in our personality or in the circumstances of our lives, but how we do it makes a difference.

With self-rejection we create changes
that keep us chasing well-being.
With self-compassion we create changes
that replenish our well-being.

MEDITATION
Giving Yourself *Sweet Me*

1.   Sit comfortably where you will not be disturbed for 10 to 30 minutes. Close your eyes, and notice your breath. You do not need to change or control your breath; just notice it.

2.   Like dropping two pebbles into a pond and watching them fall to the bottom, silently drop the words *Sweet Me* into yourself. You do not need to feel sweet about yourself or think you are deserving; just drop the words and let them fall into you in their own way.

3.   Do not try to make anything happen in response to the words *Sweet Me*. Let your awareness rest gently within you.

4.   Notice any thoughts or feelings that present themselves, and gently drop the words *Sweet Me* into yourself again. You are not intending *Sweet Me* to change your thoughts or feelings; you are simply giving *all* your thoughts and feelings *Sweet Me* as the environment in which they get to exist.

5.   Continue gently giving *Sweet Me* to every thought or feeling until you are ready to close your meditation.

6.   Take a deep, invigorating breath or two, stretch your body, open your eyes, and slowly return to your activities.

ATTUNEMENT
Giving Yourself *Sweet Me* Quickly

After you become familiar with the Sweet Me Meditation above, you can do a shorter version when needed, with your eyes closed or open—even in the middle of a conversation! If you feel distress, notice it and then silently drop the words *Sweet Me* into yourself. Don't worry whether the distress changes or not; you're simply adding *Sweet Me* to the environment in which the distress exists. Do this for one to three breaths, longer if you wish.

You might notice a subtle increase in well-being the first time you do this attunement—or, if your awareness is not yet sensitive to that level of subtlety, you might not. Either is fine. Continue to practice this attunement in different situations, with no pressure on yourself for results. With repetition, your awareness will become more sensitive to subtlety and you will feel a gentle increase in well-being during the attunement. With even more repetition, that gentle well-being will creep into your daily life.

Our culture tends to define loving yourself as loving your personality's "positive" traits, such as caring, compassion, intelligence, strength, success, and attractiveness—and as feeling love for yourself in spite of your personality's supposedly "negative" traits, such as anger, insecurity, fear, loneliness, neediness, and failure. It is impossible to maintain that kind of self-love because it is by nature judgmental, and unstable. It occurs in the personality, which is conditional. The personality's thoughts, feelings, and judgments change according to changes in conditions, so that kind of self-love comes and goes.

A deeper definition of self-love is simply *the act of opening to the love that you are.* That love is unwavering and unconditional. It remains unlimited love regardless of changes in outer conditions or in the personality's thoughts, feelings, or judgments.

This deeper self-love involves no assessments or judgments of your personality's traits (which really are only your personality's assessments and judgments of itself). You simply open to the love you are made of and be aware that it is radiating through you in that moment. With that kind of self-love, saying "I love myself" is a variation of "I open to the unlimited love I am made of. I let it nurture and guide me."

To the degree you open to the love that you are,
you open fully to life around you and the
experiences you have come into the world to embrace.

There is no need to assess whether things are going well enough in your life for you to deserve to love yourself. The two are not related. You deserve to love yourself always, regardless of how well you seem to be doing in life, how successful you feel you are or are not, or how others feel about you.

The essence of who you are is unchanged by what you do and how you assess your life. Your essence is unlimited, unconditional love and the vitality of life itself. The challenge comes in being able to know and trust that this essence is indeed what you are made of, in every moment, regardless of whether you or other people are able to perceive it on a regular basis. Yet this essence is always there within you, and you can teach your personality to open to it.

Use your experiences as mirrors for learning. When you have the feeling in a relationship that the other person does not love you enough or love you in the way you want to be loved, stop for a moment and look at how you love yourself. Do you love yourself completely, without judgment and without limitation? Are you able to love yourself unconditionally, regardless of how others see you and regardless of whether you are everything you want to be? If not, that's a signal to open to the love that you are in your essence.

As you experience the pain of not feeling loved by another,
know that you are also feeling the
loss and heartache of not fully loving yourself.

In early childhood, most people are taught by family members and society to stop loving themselves fully, to lose awareness of the love that they are. Infants and small children automatically live from their essence. They love themselves and all beings they come into contact with: those in human, animal, and spirit forms. Children's receptors are wide open.

They receive all beings and love them all unconditionally; that is their natural state.

Yet by the age of two or so, many children have already learned to stop loving themselves completely and, therefore, have learned to stop loving others completely. The two go hand in hand. That initial loss of loving oneself is indeed the greatest pain one can experience. It is the loss of the joy of being openly and whole-heartedly present in the world. In one way or another, all pain in relationships can be traced to that loss of love for oneself, loss of that open-heartedness and the ability to share it with the world.

Each day as you go about your activities, you may want to stop several times and briefly check in with yourself. In the midst of whatever you are doing, ask, "Am I loving myself while I do this?" As you drive, think, "Am I loving myself as I drive?" When you are at work, think, "Am I loving myself as I work?" When you are speaking with someone, eating a meal, having an argument, taking a bath, or making love, ask, "Am I loving myself in this moment?"

This inquiry allows you to begin noticing how automatically you forget, over and over, the love that you are. It also allows you to consciously use each activity as an opportunity to open to greater self-love. In one breath you can silently say to yourself, "I open to the unconditional love that I am."

You will feel increasing well-being as you learn to open to this kind of self-love continuously, even when—or perhaps especially when—you are engaged in activity that is unpleasant or mundane to you. Being able to love yourself in this continuous way will assist you in opening to greater realms of awareness, both within yourself and in the world around you.

15
Letting Love Light Your Life

When your personality is out of touch with self-love, it's as though there is a war going on within you, a discord between yourself and the world, or a pattern of conflict that keeps surfacing between you and others. Or you may feel a perpetual emptiness, an inner gap that you can't seem to fill. But when your personality opens to self-love, the power of love radiates through you and transforms the quality of your life.

To envision this, let's take an imaginary journey.

MEDITATION
Letting Love Light Your Life

To begin, gently allow your awareness to move into your heart center, wherever that seems to be in your chest. Imagine that no matter what tension or restriction you feel in your body, your heart center is opening and coming to life. Imagine that it is gently radiating a beautiful vibration of love that you have never before experienced.

This vibration of love is subtle, but it carries so much of the essence of life that it has a quiet power and nothing diminishes it. No matter what else you experience, this deep vibration of love is constant. With each breath you take, this love becomes brighter and more alive within you. Give yourself a few moments to receive this gift of love as it streams throughout your body.

As you continue to notice this vibration of love, gently imagine what it would be like if this love were to radiate outward to your auric field, the energy sphere surrounding your body. Your body and the space around your body would be bathed in this love.

Remember that this love, however subtle, is not diminished by anything you can think, feel, say or do. Nothing can take this love from you. It is as powerful as life force itself—because it *is* life force—and it continues to fill your body and auric field no matter what other thoughts you think or challenges you meet. Imagine what it would feel like to go through your life with this continuous love streaming through you and around you.

Now imagine what it would be like if this love not only filled your heart, your body, and your auric field but radiated outward into your world—filling your house, your workplace, your town, spreading across the planet. Everything in your world would be bathed with this love.

You can imagine, then, that everywhere you went, you would encounter love. All people and all places would be bathed with this love. Every time you had a conversation with someone, you would see and feel this love. And nothing anyone could think, feel, say, or do would diminish this powerful vibration.

This means that every situation you encountered, no matter how sad or worrisome or painful, would always carry the energy of love with it. So if something should happen to upset you, you would also feel love; the love would be there alongside the upset feeling. And, of course, when you were happy you would feel love with the happiness. Imagine what a difference it would make! It would mean that nothing in your life would ever come to you that did not come with love. Every experience would carry with it the vibration of the very love that emanates from your heart center. What a powerful thought!

And it is a powerful reality. It is already taking place in your life this very moment and will continue to take place every day. It is already real. You simply have not noticed it most of the time. Before you took these moments to focus on the feeling of love in your heart, you were not so aware of it. Similarly, you have not been aware of the love that is permeating all of physical reality. The love has been there all along. You and your world have been filled with it. When you do notice this love, it is a great joy. This experience need not be rare; the way to create a more constant experience of this love is simply to open to it, moment by moment.

Allow yourself to want to experience the radiance of love that you are, and remember that desire often. That desire takes place at a deep level and can affect the day-by-day creation of your life if you choose to let it guide you. The power of such a true desire can assist you in opening your heart and remembering the love that is your source of life.

16

Choosing Love

Your mighty ally in opening to greater self-love is your intention. This ally will gladly serve you as you start each day, but you must give it direction. As you get up in the morning and your feet touch the floor, you can pause for a moment and say, "To the depth of my being, more than anything else today, I choose to experience the love that I am." Also choose to remember that phrase from time to time throughout the day. With such clear intention, all experiences of that day will be aligned toward expanding your self-love.

Of course, calling on your ally does not necessarily mean that only pleasant things will happen to you that day. It simply means that whatever does happen—whether you like it or not, whether it is comfortable or uncomfortable—will serve the purpose of bringing you into greater self-love. Naturally you will have some experiences in life that feel painful or uncomfortable. But when you have aligned with the purpose of embodying greater love, even those difficult times will, in the end, bring you that love.

You hold yourself back when you say, "I want more love in my life, but I am not willing to go through difficult experiences to get it. I only want pleasant experiences." That limits you. Love is present everywhere, and to embody complete love of self you will face a full range of life's experiences.

Being willing to open to total love means
being willing to open to all of life.

Sometimes growth into love takes place under the surface, and you do not see evidence of it right away. You may not consciously know when an experience, either pleasant or unpleasant, has just opened you to greater love. It may take time as the love works its way into your personality's awareness where you can consciously feel it. New patterns begin long before you can feel or see them; you do not have control over the process of love's emergence.

Have faith. As you repeat your intention to open to self-love, you can trust that the work will be done. Your learning will be guided by the very source of love deep within your being that you are calling into your life. You cannot have a more trustworthy guide. Every situation and experience will automatically be fertile ground for the growth of this love. In doubtful moments, it may strengthen your trust to remind yourself of your commitment: "I want greater love in my life. I open to greater self-love, and I willingly receive the experiences that can bring it to me."

17
Loving Others

Loving yourself increases your love of others. You may have been taught to skip loving yourself and go straight to loving others, as though it is "right" or "good" to love others more than yourself. Ironically, it is impossible to be successful at this effort. Love of others cannot truly be learned or experienced unless there is already love of self.

Self-love is the basic pool you draw from for all other forms of love. When you allow yourself to be bathed with the love that you are, that love automatically emanates into the world.

*Self-love is the source that gives you
the ability to love other people.*

Your capacity for love of others naturally deepens as your love of self grows. When you know and love yourself, you spontaneously gain the ability to know and love all beings around you. So, any difficulty you have seeing others in their essence is a reflection of the difficulty you have seeing your own essence.

When you want to love others more, when you wish your heart could be bigger and your judgments less quick or less harsh, remember that what you really want is to be more in touch with the essence of your own being. You need to open your heart more to yourself. Nourish yourself first with your love, and that love will grow outward.

When you insist on seeing or loving others more fully than yourself, it is a tremendous strain. It means that your outer relationships must be lived in a way you are not living inside: You must keep giving to others what you are not giving to yourself. If you are not loving yourself, it takes tremendous energy to love others, and you must be vigilant at it. Because that love is based on effort rather than on natural emanation, you cannot stop trying to love for a moment or the loving will stop. Sometimes that loving will collapse despite your best efforts, leaving you exhausted until you recover enough to rev up the loving again.

Yet when you truly love yourself, love for others follows in a way that is continuous, natural, and effortless. Then your life is blessed, and your love is the blessing you share with the world.

18
Recognizing True Love

Relationships with other people can be complex. You often have to assess others' intentions. "Is this person honest with me?" Is it safe for me to be close with this person?" "Does this person really love me or have my best interests at heart?" How can you judge these things accurately? You may feel at risk for being fooled, disappointed, or hurt.

When self-love is real to you, you are less frequently deceived by others. It becomes clearer when others are (and are not) operating from a place of love and honor. Carrying the energy pattern of love within you enables you to recognize a matching pattern in others.

It's when you are unfamiliar with self-love that you genuinely need to be protective. Without self-love you do not carry the energy pattern of true love within your conscious experience, so you don't have a reliable standard by which to assess other people. In such situations, realize the limitation you are working with; then turn your focus from others to yourself and open to self-love. Say, "I open to deep self-love I know I can trust. I open to the love that I am." Empower yourself. In the long run, self-love will bring you the love you want from others as well as the ability to recognize it.

19
Love and Physical Reality

Some people pass through a phase in their spiritual growth of holding a negative view of the physical realm, as though it is a spiritually backward place to be. They, often unconsciously, consider themselves and others spiritually inadequate for being in physical bodies in the physical world. They may believe that the only beings who would live in the physical world are the spiritually underdeveloped ones who cannot "make it" in the higher realms, those who have not evolved enough to leave the physical realm once and for all and live as pure spirit. They may also complain that spiritual growth is slow in physical form and that physical reality itself is dense and limited. In short, they feel that the physical realm is an inferior place to be.

This condition is a spiritual version of low self-esteem in which the personality's self-rejection is projected into spiritual beliefs. In true self's perspective, however, no reality is better or worse than another because all realms are made of and infused with the same pure spirit and life force.

Physical reality is a magnificent reality
in spite of how limited it feels.

Beings of pure light and love choose to incarnate into the physical realm because it holds such rich experience and challenge. When such beings come into physical form, they open to experiences in the physical realm for the purpose of divine growth. That growth is about learning to find love even in the seeming density and limitation that characterize physical reality and the prevailing consciousness here.

It is out of love for yourself that you have chosen to come into physical form. And it is out of that same love of self that you continue to be here: researching, experiencing, creating, experimenting, and growing. Likewise, when you leave the physical realm, it will be out of love of self that you move on when you are ready.

Whenever you move from one form of reality to another, the motivation for the leap always comes from love of self. Love of self is the fuel, the power that moves you from one realm to another. So the fact that you are here in physical reality at all is proof that you loved yourself enough to make the journey. The trick now is to continue loving yourself while you are here.

The only true injury in life occurs by
going through an experience
and not being able to find the love in it.

Part of the journey you are making through physical reality involves learning to find love in the midst of every situation, every feeling, and every belief you encounter. For example, grief or loss is an intense, often unbearable emotion. Yet as you allow yourself to surrender deeply to that feeling, at the core of it you will come upon a ray of light that is love, and that will be the healer. You will find that love at the core of grief because grief, like everything, is made of love.

Finding that love will not take away the pain. It may not even take away the feeling of grief or loss, but it will transform it. At that point, feeling grief or loss can no longer deny you the experience of love.

Love and life are one and the same. Vibrationally, love is the very substance of life. No wonder it is so frightening to be out of touch with love—that means being out of touch with life and the being that you truly are. You may fear criticism because you fear not loving yourself.

You may fear your anger because you fear not being able to love others. When love is fragile and elusive, fear arises in many forms. But as you increase your ability to experience the love that you are, and the love that is at the core of every emotion, you will find less and less in life to fear.

ATTUNEMENT
Self-Love #1

Three times a day, stop for one to five minutes to remember the love that you are. If you are sitting, sit with awareness that you are opening your heart to pure love radiating through you. Imagine that love filling you and radiating outward. While you are walking, be aware of that inner radiance of love with each step. While you are talking with someone, remember that inner radiance of love at different times while you are speaking *and* listening. In every circumstance, as this love fills you it radiates into your daily life.

ATTUNEMENT
Self-Love #2

When you are in bed at night waiting for sleep, imagine that love emanates from your heart center through your body. If you use words, just use them long enough to get in touch with the subtle feeling or image of the love that you are. You might gently speak or think a phrase like "I open to the love that I am" or "The true love and light of my being radiates through me." Allow yourself to receive that love and light, however slight it may seem. Notice that feeling, letting it grow as it moves you into sleep.

VIVIAN

Vivian had trouble picturing a future with her in it. She thought it was because she had cancer and, even with the treatment she was undergoing, had been given a poor prognosis. But her problem was bigger than just her uncertain future: Vivian wasn't in her present.

She was physically there, sitting on the couch across from me in my office. The scarf wrapped securely to cover her chemotherapy-induced baldness attested to her vulnerability and struggle. Yet she had lived so much of her life for other people's approval that she didn't know or trust herself. Saddest to me was that she didn't feel she deserved goodness unless she made other people happy. Her own happiness eluded her. Receiving goodness without sacrificing for it—and feeling joy, self-compassion, or quiet well-being just because she existed—were foreign ideas to her.

I asked Vivian how she nurtured herself, and she looked at me blankly. "I'm a perfectionist. I...I just always try to do the right thing," was the only answer she could find.

"Being perfect is a recipe for depletion," I suggested, and, to my surprise, her eyes lit up. Suddenly we were on ground she recognized.

"Depletion! Yes, depletion. Boy, do I know about that. I've felt depleted as long as I can remember." She sighed, relaxing into the familiar, as though we were talking about one of her friends.

Later in the session I asked, "Vivian, if, by magic, it was totally okay for you to want as much goodness for yourself as possible, what would you want the most?"

She thought a long moment, and then words charged out as though they had been trapped underground and had just found a passage to air. "Freedom. Autonomy. Not looking to others for approval. My own voice. Speaking from my heart and soul. Not being driven by perfection—being motivated by joy and life. I want to trust higher good. I want to live. I want to thrive!"

"Wonderful. And if you had all that plus total health and well-being at every level—body, heart, and soul—what would you call it?" I asked.

"Hmmm...," she answered slowly, her eyes unfocused and dreamy, directed somewhere behind me. "Radiant health. Yes, radiant health."

We sat quietly, letting her words settle in the room.

As Vivian's eyes shifted back into focus on me, fatigue fell like a shadow over her face. With a little shrug suggesting futility she assumed was obvious to us both, another sigh escaped. Unaware of how illogical her comment would sound to me, she concluded, "But if I get radiant health, then I'll be responsible to give talks about how I did it. You know, to help and inspire other people."

Sadly, Vivian did not recognize that recovering from a life threatening disease—and on top of that, gaining radiant health she had never enjoyed, even before her illness—might be a profound and well-deserved accomplishment in itself, something purely to rejoice about and to let other people help her celebrate.

In contrast, her conclusion reflected the belief she had walked into my office with: *Her own existence wasn't valuable. She had to give more than she received. Improvements to her life had to be offset with more sacrifice to improve the lives and well-being of others. Feeling depleted was a sign she was on the right track, living as she should.*

Sometimes, like Vivian, we don't realize how ingrained our personality's beliefs of "not deserving" are or how automatically they prevent us from receiving the goodness we want. Yet eventually we have to make a choice: depletion or vitality. It is the key to revitalizing our body and regaining the joy of living. Opening to the love that we are and practicing self-compassion nurtures us, softens the grip of depleting beliefs, and teaches us how to receive goodness from ourselves, other people, and Life.

CHLOE

In 2002 a tiny, four-legged teacher bounced into my life. Chloe was a two-month-old Yellow Labrador and Golden Retriever mix who showed me what real self-love looked like. She was my first puppy, and I was enthusiastic about teaching her the basics. House-breaking and Sit came first, as well as Down, Stay, and Back (out of the cupboard or fridge—an early necessity!). She learned fast, thinking all the commands were fun games.

Our hours together on the hill in the backyard taught me some of *her* values, too. "Take time to stop and eat the flowers." "Walk softly and carry a big stick...or any stick you find." And "The grass is really a salad bar." With that groundwork laid, my biggest lesson was about to come.

One wall in my bedroom held a full length mirror. I walked by it a dozen or more times a day, every time I entered or left the room. Each pass was an opportunity for quick self scrutiny. Like a frog I once saw on Animal Planet who flung out its tongue and snatched a bug so fast I couldn't see it happen until it had been replayed in slow motion, my mind flung out tiny lashes of judgment with such speed I couldn't see how they diminished my self esteem. "I look fat." "Bad hair day." "New wrinkles." "Would a face lift really be so politically incorrect?"

Then one day as Chloe and I left the bedroom, she noticed herself in the mirror for the first time. Her reaction was simple: She paused, gave her little face a quick lick, right on the mirror, and walked on.

I was stunned. With one quick lick of her puppy tongue, Chloe had caused the frog tongue of my mind to be replayed in slow motion. For the first time, I saw what it had been doing. It had *not* been using my mirror to help me look or feel better, but to reinforce a self-image of "not good enough."

Chloe's puppy mind, on the other hand, had no self-rejection. She met herself with the same open-hearted love and acceptance she offered to everyone, unconditionally. For weeks, until her interest moved on to other things, she continued to respond to herself as the love that she was—the same love that we all are—with a quick lick on the mirror.

Part IV

JOURNEY INTO FORM

The Exploration of Limitation

20
The Journey So Far

Imagine this: Your journey into this life began in a state of pure spirit and unlimited being. Before coming into physical form, your experience was not restricted by time or limited to sequential events. You lived in a fluidity and a unity in which literally all things were possible. Although you knew individuality, there was no separation between one being and another or between one thing and another. Everything and everyone was recognized as expressions of your expansive being.

As unlimited spirit, you were a master of creation. The very instant you thought a thought, the appropriate form to express it manifested. The very instant you felt a desire, that desire (or perhaps its fulfillment) manifested. All your inner experience and refined emotional naturally manifested for you.

You lived in a highly creative state. No thought was just a thought, no feeling just a feeling. Every experience was an impulse of creative force. Because you were not in a physical body or in physical reality, all forms were more subtle, more fluid than anything physical. Yet they were real. And because your awareness was not limited by form, you were conscious at all levels. You never forgot that the manifestations you witnessed flowed from your own creative source.

Can it be that all these characteristics—unity, fluidity of time, instant manifestations, malleable form, all experienced as creative impulse, unlimited possibilities, multilevel awareness—are also true about physical reality?

All the characteristics listed above (and many more) are true of the unlimited realm without any limits applied to them whatsoever. Your experience in that realm took place at a highly refined level, and the deep, distant memory of it is guiding you in this lifetime. For example, you may be frustrated in this lifetime that the things you want to manifest in your life take so long. This slowness in physical reality contrasts with a faint memory of the tremendous speed of manifesting in the unlimited realm.

In physical reality, the personality is hypnotized by solid matter.

The way your personality perceives physical reality, what seems more solid, most unbudgeable, seems most real. You define and direct your life within the constraints you observe and choose to believe in. For example, the things you do and consciously experience stay within the limits of what you think is possible—which means you don't do or consciously experience anything you think is impossible. Therefore, *impossibility* is actually the factor that shapes your reality by putting tight boundaries around it. Your belief in impossibility tells you what the limits to physical life are and where you can expect to find them. And you abide by them.

Your personality is the aspect of your being that has adapted to physical reality. It forms and carries your beliefs in limitation and impossibility and sees to it that you live according to their restrictions. You can be happy, but only to a point. You can be magical and creative, but only to a point. You can have what you want and need, but only to a point. You can break through any barrier in life, but.... Your personality's basic job is to control your unlimitedness and act as your navigator through the limited realm of physical form and set beliefs.

Living in physical reality is a much denser experience
than living in unlimited spirit—until you realize that
even in physical form, unlimited spirit is with you.

Unlimited spirit is the essence of your being, your true nature, and you have access to it whenever you choose to open to it. You may ask, "If unlimitedness is so close at hand, then why do I feel limited? Why does my personality seem so much more real than my spirit does? Why can't I seem to live in conscious, unlimited awareness on a daily basis?"

Coming into this lifetime was a process of adjusting your awareness from the realm of spirit to the realm of physical form. Whenever you move from the unlimitedness of spirit into a new realm, part of the adjustment involves acclimating to the prevailing consciousness of the new realm. As you moved into physical reality at the beginning of this lifetime, you took on the cultural consciousness that was predominant when you came in. Because you came into physical form at a time when the prevailing consciousness here was one of separation and limitation, you took on separation and limitation as your new reality to explore.

You did this in two ways: first by simply slipping into a physical body and then by being receptive to personal and cultural conditioning.

How can moving into a body affect your consciousness? The physical body is a marvelous instrument. It quite literally allows you to be here, yet it is more than just a physical container. The body is made so its vibrations precisely match the vibrations of consciousness prevailing on the physical plane. This means that your body's job is to hold your being's vibration within a range that exactly reflects the vibrational range of physical reality and the collective physical consciousness.

The body also exactly matches the vibration, or energy pattern, of the physical earth. You absorb energy from the earth with every step you take, and that energy keeps reminding your body of the proper vibration for holding your spirit's focus here. You have energy receptors, especially in your hands and feet, for making contact with the earth and for receiving its energy patterns. This energy nurtures your body and keeps it in vibrational synch with the earth and with physical reality.

From the time you were born, your consciousness has also been bombarded with mental, emotional, and experiential conditioning. You grew up in a culture that has imprinted you continuously with information about what was and was not considered real here. As you took in this information you were pressured to adopt it as your operative reality so you could fit into your family and society.

For example, most people had the experience of growing up in families in which they were not seen and honored for all of who they truly were. As infants they were not perceived as expansive beings whose unlimited spirits extended far beyond their small bodies. In early childhood they were not recognized as being completely aware and sensitive to the thoughts, feelings, and energies moving from person to person around them. In midchildhood their true self was not seen or celebrated by the people closest to them.

Instead, most children were viewed through a projection of the consciousness from which the family was already operating. Members of the family were no longer consciously living from true self and a state of unity. Their experience of true self and unlimited spirit had been dulled and replaced by a consciousness in the personality based on limitation and separation. Having forgotten their unity, these individuals saw themselves as completely separate from others rather than deeply connected to them. Having forgotten that all things are truly possible, they experienced life as a struggle against difficult odds.

So the family related from their personality and projected their personality's reality onto the children, seeing and relating to them as personalities who were also separate and limited. In response, the children learned to view themselves that way, too. They came to experience themselves as alone, no longer one with others in a deeply spiritual way and no longer consciously one with their own unlimited being. They lost touch with their true self.

It is painful for children to realize (often even in infancy) that they are not recognized for who they truly are and that, to maintain the connection and intimacy they need from the people around them, they must forget their inner truth. Their inner senses tell them, "I have come here to connect with people. For that to happen, we must share some common reality. My unlimited nature is not real to my family, my schoolmates, my teachers, and the other people I depend on. Because I do not appear real to them as I truly am in the fullness of my spirit, I will become whatever they can relate to."

Most children allow themselves to be
molded to the cultural consciousness
to achieve the human bonding they need.

The cost to children during this adjustment is that bit by bit, year by year, the rigidity of their personality is reinforced and more of their true self is put aside, lost from conscious awareness. When these children grow older and have more thoroughly forgotten their true self, they then play out the other side of that dynamic. They become adults who unconsciously encourage the new children to put aside their unlimitedness. These acculturated adults no longer recognize the essence of unlimited children as real.

Few parents realize that they do this with their children. Their experience is that they love their children and want to connect with them. They are simply unaware that they already have put much of themselves aside and are, therefore, missing much of who their children are. They are unaware of the pressure this puts on their children and, through that unconsciousness, they perpetuate the pattern. None of this is done with malice or with conscious intent, yet it is a chain reaction that has gone from generation to generation for millennia.

Something unique is happening in the world at this time. The chain reaction is slowing. The pattern of passing on an inheritance of restricted awareness is transforming into a pattern of passing on expanding awareness. People are reclaiming their forgotten, yet always unlimited, spiritual essence by Coming Home to true self. As they increasingly live from true self, they recognize true self in others and create an environment in which true self awareness can flourish in everyone's life.

True self is your link between personality and unlimited awareness.

Your personality has become acclimated to the limited consciousness accepted in physical reality and accepts it, too. Unlimited awareness is the state of pure spirit that you unwaveringly *are*. It is time for the two to merge. Because your true self is pure spirit and is conscious (and loving!) of your personality, it embraces both realities and holds the space for their union.

21
Illusion and Truth

All limitation in physical reality is illusion.

As long as you believe that any limitation is real, you will experience it as real and will find data to back up that "fact." Limitation can be convincing. It can look real, feel real, and act real. But as you open to true self, limitation softens and gives way.

Limitation is no match for unlimited being. Limitation is real as long as you believe in it and interpret it as a force that holds you back. This is something your personality does on a daily basis. However, limitation dissolves the moment it is met with unlimitedness. Unlimitedness frees limitation.

Noticing your tendency toward limitation can be frustrating. Yet even if you are frustrated about the limitations in your life, there is no need to resist or fight them. Fighting your limitations is simply engaging one illusion with a second illusion that you can fight, dominate, or eliminate the first one. The way to regain your true self awareness and to experience the unlimitedness of your being is not to go through your life attacking your limitations. It is to allow true self awareness to come into your life alongside those limitations.

Unlimitedness is the greater truth. Limitation is the lesser truth.
Greater truth transforms lesser truth.

Unlimitedness is the truth that brought you into this life; it is the truth that maintains your presence in this life; and it is the truth that will go with you as you leave this life. Bringing unlimited awareness alongside an experience of limitation will catalyze transformation. That's why, when you're feeling bad about yourself, opening to the love that you are will soften the self-judgment. It's why opening to love at the core of grief will make the grief tolerable. It's why opening to inner guidance will teach the personality a new way of perceiving the world.

Because unlimitedness carries greater essential truth than does limitation, an unlimited experience—such as the unconditional love of true self—has a magnetic-like pull that prompts limitation to restructure. Prompted by this force, limitation will restructure itself energetically into a pattern that more closely matches the unlimited experience. Simply put, limitation will shift to accommodate, and ultimately support, unlimitedness as the dominant reality.

As this happens there is a merging of energies. The energy that previously went into maintaining the illusion of limitation, as well as the energy that went into fighting or resisting that limitation, is then used to support your experience of true self's unlimited being.

22

Living a Split

The essence of spirit is unlimited love. All spiritual sight is sight with love. All spiritual thought is thought with love. All spiritual sense or feeling is with love as well. There is no experience of a truly spiritual nature that does not come through love. The personality, however, does not always feel love, for that is not necessarily the personality's job. The personality's job is to explore the experience of limitation.

All thoughts, feelings, and believes that limit you come from your personality, as do all perceptions or assumptions that anything is impossible. According to your personality's perspective, successful living means knowing the limitations of yourself, others, and the world and focusing your creative efforts within those confines.

In your personality's experience, there are limits to everything, including the amount and conditions of love available within yourself, others, and the world. Because of this apparently limited supply of love, your personality is prone to being separated from love easily, often simply by the words or actions of other people. So it makes judgments, holds grudges, and harbors resentment. In that state of alienation from the unlimited love of true self, it is lost in its own reality.

Rest assured that the essence of your being is not affected by the limitations of your personality. Unlimited love, compassion, wisdom, and creativity continue to be your true state. From this essence all elements of your life, including your personality, are designed to give your soul the greatest opportunity for compassionate learning. Your guide through this learning is your true self.

Why does your guide seem so elusive? Your true self is fully conscious of itself and of the totality of your being, including your personality. Yet your personality is not very conscious of true self because your personality's reality does not include true self.

When your primary identity is with your personality, your personality's reality is most real to you in your everyday life. Your conscious awareness may occasionally open to the expansiveness of true self and spirit, but it usually snaps back like a rubber band to the limitation of personality. Because you experience these two realities as separate rather than integrated, it is as though you are living a split.

True self is continuously present.
It communicates with your personality at all times
but speaks in a quiet voice.

Because your personality turned its ear away from true self to adapt to the physical world it is no longer so consciously attune to the subtlety of true self frequency. It identifies with denser experiences, so your conscious awareness is accustomed to your personality's louder, more obvious voice. Your personality tells you that whatever is loudest, densest, most obvious, and has the strongest sensations is most real—and that whatever is quietest, most subtle, least noticeable, and has the least sensations is least real. True self's voice is like a faint whisper and speaks through subtlety and refined experience. Usually your personality does not recognize it.

You may be entering a phase in your life when your orientation to the two seemingly separate realities of personality and true self is shifting to one of increasing awareness of true self's presence. In this phase you are developing the ability to listen to true self and take action based on its guidance. True self's whispers are heard through your intuition, and actions you take from this source change your life.

The personality has become well developed in the current culture. This maturity of the personality brings us to the brink of expansion into a new identity. We have gone as far as we can go by identifying so strongly with the personality. We have lived the reality of personality so fully that we have completed that cycle of evolution and are now ready to move on. In fact, for survival we *must* move on to greater awareness. Because of its basis in limitation, the personality has created so much distress and so many survival crises, at the global level as well as in our individual lives, that we must make the shift to true self awareness to realize solutions. We need to draw from a more expanded and creative perspective to meet our challenges.

This is no accident. Whenever a collective consciousness completes its "study" of a particular level of awareness, it finds itself somewhat off-balance. This is natural and guarantees a built-in momentum and motivation for breaking through into the next level of reality to be explored. The natural state of imbalance brought on by having so fully identified with the personality now pushes us forward into a new identity, collectively and individually.

This identity comprises a merging of the two identities we have been ricocheting between. As this merging progresses, we will feel less and less forced to choose between limitation and unlimitedness; they will no longer be like oil and water, but together will become a new substance.

In this process neither reality wins over the other, and neither reality loses any of its characteristics. Personality simply opens to true self, and they become integrated.

Many people still think being on a spiritual path means fighting the personality and that enlightenment means defeating the personality once and for all, as thought spirit is somehow set free in that "victory." But in truth, spirit has never been imprisoned by the personality, not even for a moment. (Unlimitedness is never limited by limitation.) Spirit has only loved the personality, endlessly bathing it—as it bathes everyone and everything—in the love and light of unlimitedness.

If you want to be enlightened, be just that: in light.
Shine the light of love and acceptance
into every part of your being, as you already are.

Cherish your personality. You do not always have to identify with it or be restricted by its limited awareness, but honor it as an expression of your creative life force. Your personality has done an excellent job of showing you the reality of limitation and is worthy of your love and acceptance.

Cherishing your personality might be difficult if you feel that it controls you. You might think that if only you could get rid of your personality by defeating it or walling yourself off from it, you would be free to soar the spiritual heights you long for. But ironically it is *your personality* that thinks that!

The truth is that your personality does not control you; you identify with it. That is an important distinction to make. As you grew up you forgot true self to the degree needed to fit in with the people around you. By that process, you chose to identify with your personality as the dominant reality. It was choice. And it is still choice.

The reason this distinction is so important is that whatever you choose to identify with appears most real to you. You make your personality's reality real in your life by choosing it. If you choose to keep identifying with your personality, limitation and separation will continue to be the building materials of all situations and experiences in your life.

There is nothing wrong with identifying with your personality. It is genuinely a fine way to live. Personality is as divine as true self, and limitation is as divine as unlimitedness. If, however, you are uncomfortable with the confines of limitation and find yourself yearning for more expansive experiences, you can choose to identify with unlimitedness as well. It doesn't have to be "either/or." You can choose to identify with unlimitedness *in addition to* limitation. Remember, bringing in the greater truth alongside the lesser truth will catalyze transformation on its own.

Choosing what you identify with is done over and over every day. Each issue you face brings you the opportunity to make a conscious and sincere choice to open to true self.

Everything in this book is about inviting true self to be real in your life. You can use this book as a manual for reminding yourself to be purposeful—and creative—about directing your intention and choosing your reality.

23
Choosing Your Reality

The new reality is the merging of unlimitedness and limitation, formlessness and form, in your awareness. What will it mean for you personally? For the planet as a whole? The way to find out is to keep living and paying attention.

All people are preparing, consciously or unconsciously, for dramatic changes in their lives. For some the change may come slowly and for others quickly, but for everyone it is dramatic change. No one is free from this change because the entire consciousness of the planet is making the shift.

Your consciousness is manifested externally in your life.

As your consciousness shifts, the external manifestations and experiences in your life that were created from your old consciousness will restructure to reflect the shift. This is something you have no choice about at the personality level. Your true self is already guiding you through the life changes that come with this expansion and growth.

Your challenge during these changes is to allow yourself to shift intuitively to a more refined level of experience, including more refined sight and hearing, and more expansive perceptions of the world around you. Then you will be in synch with the change.

To the degree that your personality resists your transformation, you will have difficulty. Understand that there is nothing wrong with this resistance; resistance is part of the personality's expression. You do not need to fear your difficulties; they will not defeat you, and they do not necessarily mean you are off track. They are simply reflections of your inner struggle. Use those reflections as reminders to be patient and caring with yourself.

Just as there is no value in fighting the illusion of limitation, there is no value in fighting the personality's resistance. You can, however, benefit by allowing your personality its struggle and by extending compassion to it. Alongside personality's struggle, open your awareness to true self and the love that you are. You can be aware of your personality and true self together, side by side.

In other words, live the split. Allow yourself to be aware and accepting of both the limited and unlimited aspects of your being. Recognize personality's familiar thoughts and feelings, its old ways of being. Notice its fears and resistance to your movement into the new reality. From there, gently open to true self by sensing its love, guidance, expansive sight, and unlimited being.

At times you will be particularly aware that you have conscious choice about whether to identify with and act from your personality or true self. Experiment with choosing true self whenever you can.

Each time you let true self guide your actions,
you strengthen your ability to live in unlimitedness.

There may still be times when you do not seem to be quite ready or able to act from true self. You may catch yourself automatically operating from the habituated responses and beliefs of personality. That is all right, too. Just be conscious about it. Be honest with yourself about what you are doing; staying aware allows new growth to come to you in those situations. Then acknowledge that true self is there, patiently and compassionately waiting for the time when you can allow it to be of greater service.

The transition from personality to true self is progressive rather than sudden, a weave rather than a sharp cut. Don't worry if your growth doesn't seem fast enough. You will have innumerable opportunities to open to true self. You are supported in this process more than you know.

24

Emanations of Light

You are connected at a deeply spiritual level to all people who share your desire for spiritual growth. You are also connected to a vast collective of very wise and loving, nonphysical spirit beings who assist you in your growth. In fact, you are recognized, loved, and supported, in the totality of your being, by an unlimited number of beings of light and love in every moment. These beings are in a state of absolute alignment with the source of all life. They have no limit in their access to expanded consciousness and no limit in their ability to radiate that consciousness to others. They are aligned in pure, unconditional love.

When beings are in this state of alignment, their energy is automatically available to all who aspire to unlimited awareness. These fully aligned beings never tire of giving. Giving is their joy, their natural ability.

Just as water experiences no effort or fatigue in flowing,
pure spirit does not tire from giving to you.

These beings completely support you in your spiritual transformation and are continuously emanating waves of light to the collective consciousness of our planet. These waves of light carry energy patterns that exactly match the energy patterns of your true self. Your true self recognizes this energy and receives it, reminding your whole being of your unlimited nature and the love that you are.

You accept these emanations by choice. People who genuinely are not interested in remembering the unlimitedness of their being in this lifetime will ignore these waves of light. They will go about living their lives in whatever other ways they have set up for their greatest growth.

However, most people are, at a deep level, quite interested in standing up and receiving these emanations. You may even sense that your own longing for expanded awareness is so strong that not only are you standing up, but you are waving your arms and shouting, "Over here! I'll take more light! Over here!" Your spiritual enthusiasm is shared by countless others.

As each wave of light is received within the group consciousness, it generates a pull on the source so that the next wave of light is then released. When that wave is received, it also generates a pull for the next one, and so on. This creates a natural flow of waves of light, each bringing with it a more accelerated and expansive consciousness for the person receiving it. Because each wave must be fully received before it exerts a pull on the next wave to be release, the flow can never out-pace your ability to assimilate the light into your life. The flow is in harmony with you and cannot stimulate growth too quickly or too slowly.

In every moment the love of true self emanates through you into your life, where it creates experiences that remind your personality who you truly are. For example, your beliefs and the situations in your life may have been created by identifying with your personality. When you continue to identify with those beliefs and situations, usually unconsciously, they can act like mental or emotional blocks that keep you feeling stuck or unable to live your true potential.

As you are ready, the love of true self streaming through you will activate those blocks more intensely to prepare them for transformation. When you don't understand what is happening, those activated blocks can seem more powerful than ever. Yet, as you allow yourself to experience and move through the blocks, opening to true self and the love that you are, those blocks will be transformed into energy that ultimately supports you in living from true self.

This inner transformation will bring change into your outer life to the degree that you need it. If you have based your life on who you thought you should be or on other people's images of you, rather than on who you truly are, your whole life will change in a sequence orchestrated by your true self to set you free. You will be prompted to make new changes that reflect your true nature. Although the changes can be difficult, painful, or frightening at times, they lead to your greater fulfillment. The more you open to your true self guidance, the clearer that orchestration will be.

During these changes it may seem to you that some (or all) of the structures in your life are collapsing, or at least shaking: your work, your relationship, your friendships, and your basic view of self and the world. Your personality may have feelings of fear, loss, despair, helplessness, and failure. Your true self's perspective, however, may be that there is nothing wrong and no such thing as real loss or real failure. From true self's greater perspective, underlying all the changes you still have an unwavering source of love and well-being within you that is accessible any time you open to it—and your life will be reconstructed from your true self, this time reflecting who you are instead of who you are not. That is the stability beneath the change.

> *When you have a life that is based on who you truly are,*
> *no amount of change can shake you,*
> *and no amount of uncertainty can cause instability.*

Your stability is no longer based on holding onto life in static form and trying to keep change from occurring. Instead you have the greater strength of being able to live from your true self no matter what is changing around you and within you. Throughout this transition, all your thoughts, feelings, and actions that carry intent toward greater spiritual growth are instantly supported by spirit. You can draw upon this support whenever you desire it.

Do not underestimate the power in your desire for support and assistance. *Every* request from the heart is received instantly and assistance is always given. Always. When a genuine plea for greater growth goes out, beings of light and love, your true self, and the essence of all existence automatically respond and assist.

Assistance and guidance are given to you through the experiences of your life. Assistance may come in ways you request or expect. Or it may come in altogether different ways, through a set of experiences you would not have thought to ask for. You can never know for sure what forms (or timing) the assistance will take, but it always will arrive according to what serves your greater purpose.

Keep in mind that in reaching "outward" to spirit for assistance, you are also, naturally and automatically, reaching inward to the unlimited spirit of your own being. In this way, as you ask for spirit's assistance, you simultaneously align with your true self. The source of your assistance only appears to be external.

Outer spirit guidance serves as training wheels
for your awareness. Your own unlimited being is
the true vehicle that propels you forward.

The miracle is that when you open to true self, your unlimited nature becomes more real to your personality. Your true self is aware that it is of the same essence as all things and all beings, earthly and otherwise. That connectedness by being One is unity consciousness. As you open to true self, that state of unity emerges into your conscious awareness, and you experience your oneness with everyone and everything in the world around you—and beyond.

People whom you previously had seen as adversaries are now seen at the unity level as companions. Previously overwhelming difficulties now seem to be simply ways of receiving the vitality of life. All opposition, judgment, and separation dissolve into one shared, unlimited essence. When your conscious awareness is rooted in true self, your connectedness to all things and all beings is real to you. There is nothing and no one that is not you. And making a change in your world is as simple as making a change in yourself.

MARJORIE

"Deep, unresolved grief has been in my family as long as I can remember," Marjorie reveals to the true self class, "and depression. I was raised with the message that everything is sorrow, but you cover it up with fear—fear of the world. Something bad was always expected to happen. Instead of a world of 'goodness', I was raised in a world of 'fear of badness'. Badness was the norm."

Her voice sounds resigned, as though used to carrying the weight of her past alone. Marjorie continues, "My brother tended to be angry so I took the role of peace maker, but underneath I really felt sad, angry, and unfulfilled. Since childhood I've always been the one who placates, the pleaser, the good girl, the one who tries to keep everyone feeling okay—everyone other than myself, of course. Who I am has gotten lost. To cope, I've learned to retreat."

Marjorie's energy is low, but her authenticity is riveting. Usually timid and reluctant to talk "too much", say anything "too depressing", or take up "too much time", she has a history of holding back, not letting us know the full degree of her suffering. Now her talking so freely and deeply about herself is a gift. We listen carefully as she continues.

"There was love in my family but no joy. Now, as an adult, even after years of therapy, there's no joy in my life. I don't remember ever having joy or what it might feel like. In fact, right now I find it hard to think of *anything* that brings me joy."

She pauses, and then confesses, "I've created a similar household of fear, depression, and no joy for my son. I'm afraid I'm passing it all on to him. That's heart breaking for me." This background is emerging because Marjorie's brother, from whom she has kept distant, caught her by surprise in a conversation yesterday, verbally lashing out with judgments and accusations she feels she didn't deserve.

"My brother's anger startled me and jolted my body," Marjorie continues. "I felt hurt, sorrow, and blamed by him. His accusations about things I had supposedly said and done years ago seemed distorted and unjust.

"Yet I did what I always do in that situation with my family, and with anyone else who gets upset with me—I took the blame. His treatment of me felt unfair, but I automatically blamed myself anyway. I didn't stand up to him, outwardly or within myself. I felt his anger coming toward me, and I took it in, absorbing it and feeling awful."

I ask Marjorie what she wants to feel instead of awful. "Safety," she begins.

"Before you continue," I interject, "let's pause with *safety*. Every time you name a feeling you want, a tap root of energy instantly finds that feeling where it *already exists* unconditionally within you, in true self. It happens so subtly that it's easy to overlook.

"As you tell me each feeling, give yourself some silent time so you can consciously receive it. Assume the feeling you've named is rising from true self through that tap root, filling and nurturing you. The feeling might be very subtle, even microscopic, because it's coming from deep within you. That's okay. Receive it and enjoy it, no matter how subtle or tiny the sensation.

"Start again with *safety*, and after you feel the safety for a while, do the same with the other feelings you want."

Marjorie closes her eyes and slowly repeats, "Safety." She takes a deep breath, releases it, and is quiet as she opens inwardly to safety.

After several moments, Marjorie names the next feeling she wants, "Joy." Her breathing slows as she waits for the tiny, delicate vibrations of joy, the joy she thought she didn't have, to gently fill her.

Next Marjorie quietly announces, "Strength." Her posture adjusts— curled shoulders roll back and her spine lengthens slightly upward, like a plant greeting morning light.

"Creativity." Marjorie's voice is still quiet, but a new vibrancy is awakening within it. I wait during her silence.

"And my true spirituality." After just a brief pause, a burst of sentences breaks free, "I want to be comforting and compassionate toward myself. I want to allow myself to discover the goodness in me and around me. I want to feel that it's okay for me to discover my own desires and preferences."

Often when we say we want something, we are really saying that we don't have it—and *can't* have it. We are reinforcing our lack. If someone responds by trying to tell us how we *can* have it, or that we already have it more than we think we do, we argue or try to convince them they are mistaken. Ironically, while the other person shows interest in our *having*, we remain fascinated with our *not having*. As long as we hold that position, we are not receptive to the goodness we want.

Yet, other times, we say we want something as a way of opening a door to it, becoming more receptive, and beckoning it into our life. That's what Marjorie is doing.

To deepen her receptivity, I suggest that she let herself sink into feeling each of her phrases as I say them back to her. She nods, eyes still closed, and I begin, "Comforting and compassionate toward myself." I pause, giving her time to receive her true self's deep, subtle feelings of comfort and self-compassion as they rise to her awareness.

When she nods that she has been feeling them, I continue, "Goodness in me and around me." I wait, enjoying the new openness I sense in Marjorie. When she nods again, I add her final phrase, "My own desires and preferences."

Until now, all these qualities Marjorie wants have been present deep within her, unnoticed. The way fish idling at the bottom of a rushing mountain stream go unseen by someone standing on the bank, Marjorie's personality couldn't see through its constant rush of distress and self rejection to the calmer, abundant depths of true self. Today she is calming the water and peering under the surface.

When Marjorie nods that she is ready, I continue, "I want you to imagine something with me. Imagine that the substance that makes everything, even words, is nurturing life force. *All* words, no matter their meaning, are made of nurturing life force and, therefore, are little carriers of it. With this image, let's revisit your conversation with your brother.

"Yesterday your ears heard a string of hurtful and unfair words, but right now let's see those words as a string of tiny formations of nurturing life force coming through the air to you. Your brother related to the *meaning* of the words, using them to criticize and blame you. But now you're relating to the words in a deeper way. At the true self level, the real purpose of the words is to carry nurturing life force to you. That is the purpose of everything.

"With each breath, take in the nurturing life force carried in the words. As each word arrives, no matter its meaning, its nurturing life force gives itself to you, helping you to be kinder to yourself."

I pause to give Marjorie time to find her way into this new perspective. When I sense she is ready for me to speak again, I add, "Each word makes you feel kinder and sweeter to yourself, and more trusting of your goodness, than the word that arrived before it."

Marjorie continues silently, letting yesterday's words transform from harmful to healing. Then, with a long exhale, she volunteers, "I feel stronger about myself."

Her chest expands with a fresh intake of air, and she says slowly, as the awareness awakens within her, "This feels like pure being. It's a simple, easy state. I'm just being. Nothing's causing it—it's just my natural state of being." She is quiet again.

A few moments later, eyes still closed, she elaborates, "It's fundamental, primal. I feel this is the formless state I came into the world with. It's just pure being. I can tell that I had it up to age one or two, prior to defining who I was, before so much of my personality got formed. It was my original feeling state!

"It's a relief to uncover it and know, by feeling it, that this pure being was the state I started with. Now I want to nurture it, not cover it up any more." She opens her eyes and looks at me with calm certainty, "I can still have this pure being state. It's *me*."

"Yes, you can still have it," I agree, "and it is you. Now, while you're here talking to me in your pure being state, think of the world. Tell me what it is like to be in your pure being state and think of the world."

"I feel like I'm starting all over as an infant," Marjorie answers. "I want this original, pure being state—the state I began this life with—to remain strong, safe, and creative for me. I want *it* to define me and my life now, not externals like other people and circumstances."

Marjorie and I talk about how she might support this important choice in her daily life, and she comes up with a standard: *If something doesn't make me feel as good about myself, as whole and as safe in the world, as this original, pure being state, I won't take it as an imprint or let it define me.*

The next day I get a phone call from Marjorie. "I am amazed. *Amazed.* I've got to tell you what happened to me today. First, I have to mention that yesterday, a few hours after class, I meditated on my original, pure being state. Then this morning I woke up feeling connected with it.

"Second, you have to know that for the past three years I have felt awful about a situation in which I really let down a client. She had hired me to do a project that took me to her office a lot. All was good in the beginning, but then my client's office manager started being rude to me. His rudeness escalated into undermining my work and my positive relationship with my client. I didn't know how to stand up for myself or handle the situation. I became more and more intimidated by the office manager until finally I couldn't muster the courage to go back there. Instead I retreated, procrastinating so long that I didn't finish the job. Without even telling my client or giving her a reason, I just faded away. I had always been responsible and professional before, so I felt terrible about how I handled this situation.

"Finally, after several months, I returned to the company to apologize to the client, but I never got to say a word. As soon as I walked into the client's office, she snapped at me, 'Don't say *anything*. I don't want you to ruin my day. Just get out!'

"Even though I had been in the wrong, I hadn't expected her to be so mean. I didn't know how to respond, so I didn't speak up for myself or try to diffuse the conflict. I took in all her bad feeling about me and left feeling weak and awful. For three years I let it all fester inside me and continued to feel awful. I also became afraid of running into that client around town. Seeing her was my worst fear.

"Well, today it happened. As I came around an aisle in the grocery store, there she was. Her back was to me as she talked to a clerk in the produce section. She didn't see me, but I knew she might spot me somewhere else in the store.

"At first I was scared, so I took a few breaths to center myself into the state of pure being I felt yesterday in class. I felt calmer right away, and then some peace, balance, and well-being spread through my body. I decided that if she and I did come upon each other in another aisle or in the checkout line—and even if she was mean to me—I would respond from my state of pure being. My pure being felt bigger than the conflict, so I chose to put my pure being in charge.

"Sure enough, a few minutes later the woman rolled her cart next to mine. She said, 'Hello!' and was all smiles, 'How nice to see you!' Her warmth was genuine, and I instantly was happy to see her, too. Right away she told me that she had come to understand the situation differently over time, even making a point to say, 'And that office manager no longer works there.' She had extended a bridge between us, so I stepped onto it with her.

"I apologized for not finishing the job, and we talked easily, resolving the old issue and confirming our good feelings about each other. As we said our Goodbyes, she opened her arms, and we hugged.

"It felt like a miracle to me. I believe it was no coincidence that the meeting I had dreaded for three years occurred the day after I discovered my state of pure being. What an amazing synchronicity! For three years I suffered because my personality didn't know how to handle that situation. Then as soon as I found my pure being, the part of myself that *could* handle the situation, the opportunity manifested.

"And I'm proud of myself. I used that opportunity by dropping into my pure being and choosing to face my client and our unfinished business from that place in myself. In my pure being, there was no conflict, no shame, and no emotion—just different kinds of well-being. I decided to stay in that well-being no matter what happened, even if she was still mad and wanted to chew me out. I was rooted in my well-being, and the situation manifested well-being."

Part V

CREATING YOUR WORLD

Abundance and Manifesting

25

Longing for Abundance

Abundance is rich fulfillment and prosperity in all areas of your life. Satisfying the longing for abundance begins by compassionately hearing your personality's long-muffled cries for greater self-love. It requires opening your heart to a level of inner need you may have ignored since childhood.

Being without self-love creates an inner barrenness, which manifests circumstances of lack in your outer life. If your inner experience is "I cannot have love of self; I cannot have the inner richness of fully being and loving all of who I am," then the outer experience may be "I cannot have the richness of what I want most in external reality, either." So you are likely to manifest recurring situations of not having enough money or love or friendship or whatever would bring a greater richness to your life.

To heal this empty spot, you must look within. Looking within does not mean being critical or coldly tracking down your flaws to get rid of them, for harshness does not heal. Instead gently turn on an inner light, and look with tenderness and compassion to see how you can love yourself more.

Pretend for a moment that a small child whom you deeply love comes running to you, crying, and climbs onto your lap. And pretend that you can see right away that this child's problem is self-esteem, that this child does not believe that she or he is really lovable. What would you do?

Would you scold this child for lacking self-love? Certainly not. Instead, you would hold this child close and say, perhaps in different words, "I see that you have forgotten what a wonderful being you are. You have forgotten your beauty. You have forgotten your vitality, your magic, your lovability. I allow my love for who you are to fill you, to teach you, to remind you. I see who you truly are, and I love you. I hold you in this love so you can remember to love and treasure yourself."

Do the same for yourself. Be willing to hold yourself on your lap, so to speak, and look into the being that you are with that same love and compassion. Simply see where you have forgotten your own magic, where you have forgotten the love that you are and the beauty you carry within. Then make a commitment to rediscover it in some way each day.

26
Receiving Abundance

Abundance is a given in your life, but you may not know it. You may feel removed from abundance and assume it exists somewhere "out there," perhaps for other people, perhaps as something you are trying to create or attain, something you are trying to break through to.

You cannot create, attain, or break through to abundance. Like the love you are made of, abundance is an ever-present, unconditional quality of life. Abundance is radiating through you and around you already. Always. The trick is to open to it, know that it fills you, and let it guide you. Abundance is not something to get; it is something to receive.

Like the sun, abundance is unconditionally present and available to all. When you want the sun, you do not try to create it or control it. You simply step into its light and warmth and allow yourself to feel it. The same is true of abundance. Until now you may have spent your time standing in the shade, looking around and wondering, "Where's the abundance? It should be here by now. I'm working hard for it; where is it?"

It may be time to take some steps out of the shade and into the light where you can receive the abundance you have been longing for.

ATTUNEMENT
Receiving Abundance

1. Want.

Allow yourself to feel your desire fully. You may feel defeated at the prospect of feeling your desire without knowing for sure that it will be fulfilled. If your response to that feeling of defeat is to stop wanting, you also are stopping the energy to create fulfillment. You can proceed no further without reclaiming this vital energy of wanting. Fully allow all your true desires to come forward, regardless of whether they seem feasible or likely to be fulfilled.

There is a correlation between the degree to which you allow yourself to want and the degree to which you allow yourself to have. When you honestly allow the desire to grow as large as the desire itself wants to grow, you are more likely to allow the manifestation of its fulfillment. *When you open the channel of creativity on the wanting end, it will open naturally at the manifesting end as well.*

2. Feel

When desires begin to be felt fully, other feelings may surface, too. Allow yourself to feel them. Sometimes it will be sadness or despair. "I want this for myself, and wanting makes me feel sad for all the times I have not had it." "I feel barrenness in my life, of what I have been missing for so long." "It feels futile. I don't know how to get what I want, and I probably can't have it anyway." There may also be anger. "Why didn't I let myself have this sooner? I am so angry to have lived my life in this way!" Or "It's someone else's fault that I didn't get my needs met. I'm angry that they kept me from getting the goodness I wanted!" It is important that you allow such feelings—and others—to come forward to be felt and expressed. Give them compassion as they reveal themselves.

(Note: Enlist the help of a good support person, or even a therapist, if you need one. This is especially important if your feelings frighten you or might overwhelm you, if they might be difficult to contain or to express safely, or if you're tempted to take negative action toward yourself or another person. The use of feelings in this exercise is not meant to be extreme or to be disruptive to you or to someone else. Take good, compassionate emotional care of yourself, which includes reaching out for help and support when you need it.)

3. Move.

Let your body move with these feelings. Most emotion comes with an impulse to move, even if it's just facial expressions or arm gestures—or walking in a particular way: perhaps dragging your feet, stomping, or skipping. If the impulse is to cry like a child who is sad, frustrated, or angry, give yourself permission to do that. Have your support person with you if you need to, but allow your body some expression.

This is not meant to be extreme expression. What is important here is letting your feelings move through in a healthy way. The physical body is the home of emotions; it is where they live. All emotions have physical, chemical, and cellular effects. It is important to allow the *motion* of the emotions to go through the body so you can be clear, integrated, and open to new experience at all levels.

4. Trust.

Trust yourself. Trust the desires you have had, trust the feelings you have had in response, and trust the movement that has taken place. It has been real, it has been you, it has been important.

This step is a way of staying present with yourself through thick and thin, regardless of how it feels. There is a tendency in people who feel out of contact with abundance to lose contact with themselves. The two go hand in hand. When you are out of touch with yourself, you are less open to abundance that is personally meaningful and deeply enriching for you. When you remain in touch with yourself, you are more open to that abundance. That is why it is important to stay with yourself throughout this progression of experiences and to trust yourself.

5. Let Go.

Now let it go. Take a deep breath, and notice that you have completed the circuit. The active work has been done. In following steps one through four, you have given yourself a gift. You have cleared, attuned, and aligned with yourself. You need do no more.

At this point you may have your marching boots on, ready to charge forward and pursue the things you want. If that is a true desire—motion that still wants to be expressed or a healthy impulse to take steps toward reaching a goal—then follow it. In fact, often there is outer action to be taken. For example, if the abundance you want is increased financial success in your business, or a community of friends who share your passion for spiritual growth, you will need to take practical action that is in synch with the fulfillment of your desire. Take that action from the abundance-based energy moving through your body. That is empowered, abundance-based action.

However, if your personality is pressuring you to do more from a state of anxiety, or from distrust of yourself and the process you just completed, give yourself permission to let that pressure go. It is an illusion. You have done your work, and you can sit down now. You can go back about your life, watching for opportunities to take empowered, abundance-based action, and allowing yourself to receive.

6. Receive.

Allow the effects of your abundance process to come to you in your life. Allow yourself to receive what you want. Steps one through five have been the steps for moving out of the shade into the light of abundance, and step six is simply receiving it.

It may come to you in the form you wanted or it may not. The important thing is to be receptive; the essence of your desire is what comes back to you fulfilled, and you can't predict how that will happen. It may come in ordinary circumstances, words someone says to you in conversation, a chance meeting, a synchronistic event, or a change in someone's attitude and actions toward you. Or it may come as a special opportunity or an impulse you get to take a specific action. Or you may suddenly have an "Aha! moment" that juices you with inspiration and a greater perspective. Be open to recognizing and receiving the fulfillment of your desire in whatever way it comes to you.

The feeling of desire arises because you feel separate from what you want, as though a glass shield stands between you and abundance. You can see the abundance on the other side. You can occasionally see other people going up and taking part in the abundance, then turning around and telling you how to do the same. Yet the glass remains. Your work with these six steps can help the glass dissolve. Then you will begin to see that what you wanted was never far away, never separate from you at all.

27

Manifesting

You already have unlimited ability to create in physical reality. Everyone does. You are involved in the creation of physical reality all the time. At this very moment, just by being who you are, you are creating the next moment and the next and the next. You could say, for example, that the next six months of your life are created already, not as fate but as possibility, just by your being who you are in this moment.

In your essence, you are unlimited spirit who has come into physical form. Through your physical body your spirit communicates with physical reality, and through your physical body your inner creative force moves outward to the physical world to manifest. Most important to know about this process is that *your experience of self* is what creates every aspect of your life.

Everything is energy.

Physical matter is energy. Thoughts are energy. Feelings are energy. Every image, thought, feeling, and belief you consciously or unconsciously hold about yourself carries a specific energy formula or pattern to it. These energy patterns are complex and real. Collectively they make up your experience of self, which is your inner reality. This ongoing inner reality creates the outer reality you live with every day.

Your auric field is the energy space extending outward from your body. It links your inner experience with the outer world. Through your auric field, the precise energy patterns of your experience of self are transmitted outward to the physical world. They are a template for everything that manifests as your life. These energy patterns create all your outer experiences (situations, relationships, prosperity, etc.) and your responses to them. So everything you encounter in life is a reflection of your inner experience of yourself! In that way, your experience of everyone and everything is a mirror for you and is also subject to change as your experience of self changes.

Whatever you emanate, you will encounter.

If you are aware of yourself as love, for example, those energy patterns are transmitted outward through your auric field, and what you encounter in your life will be the manifested experience of that love. Then the world may seem to you a loving place, or at least a more loving place than it would seem if you were less aware of yourself as love.

If you are not aware of yourself as love and do not cherish and honor yourself, your energetic pattern of "nonlove" is transmitted outward through your auric field into the world and manifested in your life. You may encounter situations over and over in which you are not loved, honored, or treated kindly. Life can then be a frightening experience.

Consider also that your experience of self will determine what actions you take in life. If you carry conscious self-love, you will tend to take actions that are loving and will then reap more loving responses from the world.

Understand that you are not bad or flawed for not loving yourself more, only hungry for the nourishment you deserve. When you are caught in such limitation, it is always possible to open to greater experience. Remember, the change begins within you.

You alter your patterns of outer manifestations
by altering your inner experience of self.

Be willing to allow yourself greater love. Nurture self-love in spite of what life seems to be giving you or telling you about yourself. Then you automatically will be adding more self-love to your energy pattern that transmits outward for manifestation. After a period of time the world will seem to change and you will encounter more love in your life. You will begin to find yourself treated more honorably and cherished more often. You will feel more supported in outwardly living the love that is your true nature.

28

Empowering Your Desires

Your manifesting energy never stops working for you. As a highly creative and purposeful force, it literally enables you to interact with projected forms of your being everywhere you go. To whatever degree your experience of self includes inner nurturing and support, your outer relationships will show nurturing and support. To whatever degree you inwardly experience abundance, your outer manifestations will be of abundance. Yet, nothing you manifest in physical reality is important in and of itself. It is all there purely as your reflection for learning and growth. Every person, thing, and situation you encounter is symbolic of some aspect of you.

The purpose of manifesting anything is simply to make your experience of self apparent in physical reality. When you insist on manifesting something for any other purpose, you are at cross-purposes with your own nature. That in itself can be frustrating and can leave you wondering, "Why isn't what I want coming to me? Why isn't it happening?"

When you have that feeling, let it remind you to drop to a deeper level of awareness, to true self. If you find yourself being attached to having more money, a relationship, a new car, a better job, or something else, and you do not seem to be getting it, experiment with looking at the situation differently. Be aware that your desire for the thing (the money, relationship, car, etc.) is a desire from the most superficial level of your being: your personality.

Although you may be more aware of your personality than you are of your deeper levels of self, your personality carries the least power. It is the most oriented to control, has the strongest sensations, and makes the greatest demands, but it carries the least true power. Because your deeper levels of self are progressively more aligned with true self, they carry progressively more manifesting power. You can activate this greater power by simply shifting your awareness deeper. Attuning to the following four levels will take you progressively deeper: (1) Superficial Desire; (2) Essence Desire; (3) Internalized Desire; (4) Desire for True Self.

1. Superficial Desire

Each superficial desire is a symbol
for a greater desire you hold at a deeper level.

Your personality is most familiar with superficial desire, which is the desire for things (and situations) that you assume will bring happiness or fulfillment. This desire is reinforced by cultural messages that achievement, material gain, and other people are the source of your well-being and sense of self.

Of the four levels, superficial desires are noticed most frequently. Yet they take the most exertion to pursue and are the least satisfying when fulfilled. Recognizing that your superficial desires are incomplete in themselves frees you to look for your deeper power.

2. Essence Desire

You can empower yourself
by going directly to the essence of your desire.

It is easy to let your awareness drop from the superficial to the essence level by asking yourself, "What is the essence of this desire? What is the quality in my life or the experience of myself that I want from this?"

For example, money is the most common desire at the superficial level. Yet money is a symbol for many things. What is the essence level of money for you? Perhaps you believe that when money comes it will bring you ease in the world. Having your financial needs met can indeed bring a certain type of ease. Or maybe having more vacations would bring you joy. Or maybe you simply want the feeling of being supported in life.

The essence of what you want is the feeling or quality that would come into your life by getting the thing (money) that you're focused on. The ease or joy or support is always a deeper desire than the money is. And regardless of how often it may appear otherwise, *you always want the essence more than you want the thing.*

Let your personality's superficial desires serve as your springboard to the essence level. Each time you catch yourself wanting a "thing," stop and deepen the dialogue. Remind yourself of the truth. "I want more money" becomes "What is it I really want? Oh yes, now I feel it. The essence of what I really want is more peace (or ease, or joy, etc.) in my life." Or it may be "I want to feel supported in the world. I want to feel supported in being who I really am and in having what I need." When you're willing to make this shift, wanting a thing (money, relationship, car, job, or whatever) automatically reminds you of your deeper desire.

Let the essence level of desire be real to you. Allow it to become a part of your awareness every day so you can stay in touch with what you actually want. When the essence of your desire becomes real to you daily, it stimulates a shift in your pattern of manifesting. As your awareness of your essence desire integrates into your daily life, it becomes part of your experience of self and energetically supports the direct creation of what you truly want.

You can still want more money, a relationship, a car, or a new job. There is nothing wrong with wanting on the superficial level; that's part of living in the physical world. But if you assume that getting the thing will somehow make up for what you're missing at the essence level, you put yourself on a treadmill of dissatisfaction. Staying focused exclusively on the thing can enable you to get it, yet nothing will have changed at the essence level because that was not where you put your focus. You will have gotten the symbol but not the essence that the symbol represents. You will have the money you wanted, but still not have enough ease or joy or support in your life. If even then you do not change your focus to the essence level of wanting, you may soon find yourself chasing another symbol, another thing, in the hope that it will save you.

If you wonder why you never quite get what you want, look closely at that dynamic because it is basic to manifesting. Remember that you always really want the essence more than the thing. As you allow your essence desire to be as real, or more real, to you than your desire for the thing, you are well on your way to manifesting it.

3. Internalized Desire

Essence desire is wanting meaningful qualities in your life;
internalized desire is wanting them in yourself.

Internalized desire brings your focus even closer to Home. For example, if your essence desire says, "I want to feel supported in the world," you can drop your awareness deeper to the level where you want to feel more supported by *you*. "I want to feel more support for myself from myself." This support is not based on your achieving any particular outer standard of being worthy or deserving. It is a basic need for unconditional support of self—a support of self that does not fluctuate according to outer realities such as your financial situation or other people's feelings about you. Or, if you want more joy in your life, look within for the level where you want inner joy that is not taken away by changes in outer events or relationships.

4. Desire for True Self

Underlying the desires for all things and all essence qualities,
is the desire to discover your true nature.

Desire for true self goes something like this: "More than anything, I want to live from my true self so fully that I experience it in every moment, everywhere." The desire for true self is so basic that everyone has it as their deepest longing, whether they are conscious of it or not.

Fulfilling the desire for true self means that the personality surrenders to true self, with joy and relief, recognizing it as its essence and source. Your inner and outer experiences merge; all is vibrant life force and well-being. Imagine living with that awareness daily, recognizing unlimited spirit as yourself, and as everyone and everything you see. That is freedom. That is glory. That is Coming Home.

This true self state of unity means that you experience yourself as one with all aspects of your being and one with all things and all beings: human, animal, earth, spirit, and beyond. When you are in this state, you already have everything you want. And when you recognize your true self already manifested in the world, manifesting things like money, a car, a relationship, or a job becomes child's play. So don't be surprised if, in your return to true self, you lose interest in creating some things that had been important to you before. When you have learned to drop beneath the symbols to create what you've always wanted most, the more superficial desires will seem less urgent.

You may have a tendency to go for the symbols when you don't feel able to go for true self. You may not know what your true self is, your true self may seem impossibly out of reach, or maybe you simply are not aware that your true self even exists. So when you can't get in touch with the deeper possibilities, you automatically gravitate to the more superficial ones. You may even become good at manifesting on the superficial level and creating lots of things in your life. Yet you are stuck there until you choose to open to greater depths, to *your* greater depths, and plunge in.

You may find that most of your time and energy in working with manifesting the fulfillment of your desires goes into levels one, two, and three—and probably in that order. Yet it is important also to be aware of level four. Working (or playing!) with the deepening levels of desire is a way to move more intimately into yourself and to explore who you are, yet still stay connected with the outer world. You can move back and forth between inner and outer, superficial and deep, and never be in the wrong place.

There is no wrong place in this exploration. All of it is you, and all of it is valuable. Just keep paying attention. The more awareness you bring to this process, the more quickly and deeply you will learn.

29
Relinquishing Control

Your essence is love. Furthermore, all physical reality is love manifested in innumerable forms. Let's look at what this means. When you feel the emotion of love, it is easy to think of that as a manifestation of love. Yet that emotion is only the tip of the iceberg. All experiences are made of love, from the most mundane to the most unusual, and most go unrecognized for the profound potential they carry.

Any situation in your life that is difficult is as much a manifestation of love as is a pleasant one. For example, think of an experience that brought pain or other discomfort into your life. You may remember how distressing it felt and how much you resisted it. You may still think of it as a negative experience. Clearly, that situation didn't look or feel as if it was a manifestation of love, yet it was. It came to you full of possibilities for learning—graced for growth. When you genuinely recognize all occurrences as vehicles for love, a quality of richness and surrender enters your life. There is a deep connection, a sense of peace, openness, and safety that you cannot find without accepting this basic truth.

When you recognize love in all of life's experiences,
you are freed from your belief in nonabundance.

This idea may prompt you to think, "Okay, everything going on in my life is love. Some of it feels good, some of it feels bad, but it is all love. So how do I control these manifestations of love to create more good experiences and fewer bad ones?"

When you have experiences that feel comfortable, exciting, or wonderful, there is a tendency to think, "Right now things are going just as they should. Things are good." Such a belief implies that when you do not feel so good, it means that something is wrong, that things are not going well, that it is a bad situation. When you think of experiences as good or bad, positive or negative, you limit yourself and close yourself off from important avenues of growth.

From the perspective of unlimited spirit, when things are uncomfortable—perhaps you feel stuck in pain, fear, or uncertainty—nothing is necessarily wrong. You simply are embracing life as a human being in the midst of discomfort. Love is still present in that experience, no matter what the situation is or how uncomfortable it may be.

You cannot control your manifesting to the point that you create only experiences you think are positive, meaning that they feel good to you. You must allow life to present itself to you without control. It is fine to say to yourself, "I want to manifest work that reflects who I really am and gives me the opportunity to express my true self in the world." It also is fine to say, "I want to create more financial support and greater ease in my life," or "I want to have loving relationships; I want to experience an openness in my heart that I have not yet felt in this lifetime." But it is limiting to add, "...and I am not open to anything else," or to believe that everything painful or tragic is bad, or is some kind of failure by you, someone else, the world, or Life.

That type of control makes you resist some of your most potentially expansive experiences if there is pain or loss involved. A situation that causes grief, for example, is often thought of as a bad thing to manifest because it is so uncomfortable. A situation that causes extreme grief and pain is called a tragedy. Your mind may say that you would be crazy to wish for something that brings you grief or great pain. And yet, in its deeper wisdom, your true self knows that grief can cleanse the system and open the heart in a powerful way. So you may actually will an experience of grief to yourself because of all it has to offer.

Understand that you usually do not will grief (or pain, illness, suffering, and so on) to yourself at the conscious, personality level. In fact, your personality will emphatically resist such experiences and deny any part in their manifestation. But remember that your personality is the most superficial aspect of your being (the most unaware of true self) and, therefore, has the least true power. Your true self has much greater power in manifesting. It uses this power to create precisely the situations that offer your personality the most perfect growth. At that level of deep compassion and expansive insight, you will all your experiences to yourself.

Applying this concept can be tricky for the personality, who doesn't completely understand it. So it's important that you do not use the concept of "you create your reality" against yourself. If you find yourself in a distressing situation—perhaps a divorce or loss of a loved one—thinking "I created this situation" and feeling like that means something is wrong with you, that is an inappropriate use of the concept of creating your own reality. Immediately stop and give yourself compassion; open to the love that you are.

Or if you find yourself talking to a friend who is facing a distressing situation, perhaps a serious health challenge, and you are thinking, "Well, everyone creates their reality, so my friend must have willed this problem to happen", that is inappropriate, too. Again, stop and give *yourself* compassion—because even though your friend is the one with the problem, you are in distress, too.

It is a sure sign you are in distress when your assumptions about creating reality make either you or your friend flawed or deserving of distress—neither of which is true. Opening to self-compassion when you or someone else is in distress will take you deeper into your true self, which is the antidote to the personality's inability to make loving sense of a disturbing situation. Always be interested in the most compassionate and empowering ways to understand how you create your reality.

It is never appropriate to use spiritual concepts
to create feelings of blame, shame, or inadequacy
in yourself or others.

Every thought, conscious or unconscious, is powerful. By consciously directing your thoughts, you can use their power to align with true self and its guidance in your life. This alignment can be particularly effective in transforming your distress. For example, when you are facing a personality difficulty, you can stop for a moment, take a deep breath, and—without denying any of your distress—choose for that situation to be a vehicle for deep empowerment. Take a moment to affirm something like, "I open to all that I am. I align with true self and the love that I am. Through this situation, I allow the energy of my true self to move into my life."

Sometimes you will feel the effects of this affirmation immediately. Other times you may not feel anything right away. Trust the thought anyway, and pause for a deep shift to take place, even though it may be so subtle that you cannot feel it consciously. Your intention is powerful, and the shift will take place regardless of whether you feel it. Subtle shifts happen at a core level and lay the groundwork for future experiences that will noticeably match your affirmation.

If you have even the most subtle sensation that something has shifted—perhaps your spine stands just a bit taller, your facial muscles relax a little, or you have a new feeling of lightness—notice it. However subtle, however insignificant it may seem, acknowledge it. "I open to true self, and I allow the subtlety of it."

When you understand the power of such subtle experience, you take a lot less for granted in life. By attuning to the subtle inner and outer shifts that occur in response to your directed thought and feeling, you begin to understand and witness how you affect your reality in each moment.

Reality is created tiny bit by tiny bit.

Imagine that your current life, your current reality, is a great puzzle made up of microscopic pieces that you put together. Some areas are still in the process of being assembled, so the puzzle is incomplete. Each time you create a subtle shift within yourself, you take a new piece to that puzzle and press it into place. This is a self-directed way of putting your life together as you go along. By consciously choosing what you attune to, you are creating the content of the puzzle and your life.

30
Owning Your Power to Create

As you think about consciously creating your life, you may wish you were better at manifesting. Yet the truth is that you already are manifesting excellently in every moment! Just look at your life and see how much has come to you. Whether it's happiness, sadness, fear, doubt, pain, joy, or lightness of spirit, your life is a rich blend of what it is to be alive and vital and full of human experiences.

Your very ability to create in physical reality is what has enabled you to be here in the first place. A being who does not have the inherent ability to manifest would never get into physical reality. To be here you must manifest yourself into physical form. After you have done that, you naturally have the ability to manifest anything in your life, and you never lose that ability.

You are the creator of your life:
at some level you have wanted or needed
every experience you have encountered.

Recognition of this truth is a fundamental step toward more conscious manifesting. It allows you to recognize the power you have been using all along and to begin to direct it with intention. Yet you may find that you have some resistance to this idea. Believing that you have created your life and have wanted all that you've created can be frightening to your personality. Your personality often forgets that greater levels of your being are in charge.

If you are unhappy with your work and you don't have enough money to pay the bills, your personality may refuse to accept that you created such an "undesirable" situation. It may say, "I'd be stupid to create this!" It may think that taking responsibility for creating your life means having to blame yourself, as though creating such a challenging or uncomfortable situation is a negative thing.

Your personality forgets that the deeper soul of your being views your life from a different vantage point. Perhaps your personality doesn't want the situation of having a job you hate and insufficient money to cover your bills; but perhaps your soul does choose that situation. Your soul may see that through that challenge you will learn important lessons— about who you truly are, what your spiritual relationship with money is, or how clearing your issues with money can heal a deeper inner struggle.

The soul's teachings are usually much bigger
than anything the personality can grasp right away.

You may not be able to completely understand what your lesson is about until you have lived it through. That's how your soul teaches your personality—by living. So, until you have lived through the deeper teaching enough to really understand it, let yourself be unknowing! Also, let yourself surrender to the sense that, somewhere deep within, you have wanted and created each situation in your life and that you love yourself enough to open to the learning it brings.

If you think that owning your power to manifest means that you must blame yourself for your "misfortunes," see if you can open your heart to a new compassion that will gently melt the self-blame. Your manifestations are never wrong or bad. They may sometimes be uncomfortable, painful, or overwhelming, but they always are for a deeper purpose. Always.

Maybe you are used to blaming others (other people or outer

circumstances) for some of your difficulties or pain. This is a very human thing to do, and almost everyone has this tendency. Owning your power to manifest disrupts this pattern of blaming others, and your personality may respond with resistance to this change.

Three major forms of resistance may surface.

1.   Fear of Shifting the Blame.

If your personality needs to blame other people or circumstances— "He is the cause of my unhappiness." "You can't buck the system." "That's just how life is."—it will be afraid to let go of outer blame, as though its defenses are being taken away. Here the basic premise is, "It must be *somebody's* fault; if it's not their fault then it must be mine." Within that belief, if you take the blame off others it automatically falls back onto you. That feels uncomfortable, unfair, and debilitating; no wonder you resist it!

2.   Fear of Losing Your Power.

Your personality may assume that taking responsibility for creating your life means automatically letting everyone else off the hook for his or her behavior. If you hold yourself accountable, but think you no longer can hold other people accountable for themselves, it feels as though they have power and you don't. You feel weakened and forced into a passive role. No wonder you resist this, too!

3.   Fear of Being Stuck.

You may have a hidden belief that if you avoid responsibility for something uncomfortable in your life, it will go away—or at least be less real. The flip side of that belief is the fear that if you do claim what you have created and face it straight on, you won't be able to do anything about it and you'll just feel bad. You assume that you will then be stuck repeating the pattern, caught in it for good. Here again, you resist.

Ironically, in spite of these beliefs, to the degree that you distance yourself from whatever you have manifested in your life, you are likely to continue to manifest it. When you consciously or unconsciously say to yourself, "I do not want to look at my power to manifest: I do not want to acknowledge that I've created the difficulty in my life," you are likely to continue to create that very difficulty. You unconsciously create experiences over and over until you own your creation.

By rejecting the idea that you create what you have, you distance yourself from your manifesting power (which is also your creativity) and weaken your ability to draw to you what you want. Or, if you reject your current life and try to escape from it into something new, you will find that you never quite seem to get away. It is by fully embracing your current life and *loving yourself in the midst of it* that you heal what needs to be healed, that you free yourself and are empowered to create and attract something new.

> *Living is the act of surrendering to and exploring*
> *the life you already have,*
> *learning to love yourself in the midst of all your creations.*

If you completely accept that you have created your life, you embrace your creative power. Changing your life then becomes much simpler. You can look at a difficult experience and sincerely say, "It feels as if this happened to me, and it feels as if I would be crazy to want this in my life. Yet I see from the heart of my being that I manifested this. I accept that I created this experience out of deep wisdom and love for myself. I open to the learning it offers."

If you continue to be unconscious of manifesting everything in your life, you continue to feel that things happen *to* you. But as you allow yourself to acknowledge and align with your deep creative power, you free yourself to manifest more consciously and compassionately.

Another way of saying this is that when you surrender to the creator within, you surrender to having created everything in your life. *You love yourself instead of judge yourself, in the midst of your creation,* no matter how comfortable or uncomfortable your life may be. This surrender is an act of power. People who can do it need to be told very little about how to manifest.

Surrender is not just mental or emotional. It is much deeper. It is the feeling of complete immersion in the experience of yourself as creator of your life and immersion in love of yourself in the midst of your creation. This love does not necessarily mean that you love *what* you've created in your life or even that you have to be comfortable with it, but that you love *yourself* in the midst of it all. From there you will intuitively know how to create what you want for yourself in the future. In fact, as you sit in that immersion, whatever you think and deeply feel you want in your life is instantly put into the programming for future manifestation. When you have the experience of yourself as manifestor, you are able to consciously direct that manifesting ability to enrich any area of your life you choose.

31

Transforming Your Blocks

Major transitions are not always easy. It takes time to live new truths. Sometimes as you go through transformation, it seems as though every personality pattern that ever held you back becomes stronger or comes at you from a new angle. You may find yourself caught in feelings or memories of being unloved and alone. Emotional pain and despair may surface. Rigid beliefs of "I can't have" and "I don't deserve" may seem to get the better of you for awhile. You may become confused, frustrated, or doubtful that you are making progress.

It's all right if this happens. It does not mean you are losing ground or you will not be successful in your spiritual growth. It simply means that you have been willing to drop into yourself at a deeper level. This commitment to new depth is like a light that shines into the dark corners of your unconscious, flushing out everything at that level that is still holding your personality back and blocking its awareness of true self. This is your "shadow", unclaimed aspects of your personality where you have been afraid to "turn on the light" before. Now, out of self-love, you are allowing these issues to come forward into the light of awareness to be faced and embraced.

Each area of darkness is an offering
to the light of your true being.

Each transition through the darkness is a sacred rite of passage, performed from great self-love and willingness to become whole no matter what the challenge. You are moving into greater abundance; open your heart to yourself and proceed, allowing each shadow to make its way to the light as it is drawn out for healing.

In the midst of this transition, your personality's inner blocks to fulfilling your true desires can seem strong. Understand that no block is a real block; that is, no block has power of its own. A block appears strong because you experience it that way, and you believe your experience. Your blocks are the areas where your personality identifies with limitation. You can diffuse each block by inviting a deeper, more unlimited experience alongside it.

Sometimes you may feel as though your personality has the most control over you, but because it is the most superficial aspect of your being, it always has the least true power. As we have seen, the greatest power comes from the deepest core of your being: your unlimited true self. As you move inward, or deeper, from your personality, each level of awareness carries greater truth and, therefore, greater power. In other words, the more closely aligned with true self your awareness is, the more power it carries.

For example, the belief "I can't have" can remain, undisturbed, and you can still have what you want. If you allow yourself to hold two levels of awareness around a given issue, the deeper awareness will always carry more power and, over time, will transform the more superficial belief. So if you hold your personality's belief in limitation ("I can't have") alongside the deeper truth of essence desire ("I choose greater ease") or greater abundance ("I am willing to have"), the deeper truth will prevail.

It may take time and repetition—remembering to attune to the deeper level whenever a block seems to be stopping you—but sooner or later the deeper truth will transform your block. That is why you do not have to reject or fight your block. When it becomes your habit to open to the deeper level, your block will be transformed naturally by the greater power of the deeper truth.

Truth always transforms nontruth.

The truth of your being is a brilliant light that will shine into the shadows of your personality, transforming the dark to light whenever you offer those shadows to it. You make your offering with your awareness. When you recognize a limiting belief or desire, let your awareness move to a deeper level, to a greater belief that already exists along with the limited one or a deeper desire below the superficial one.

As the greater truth transforms the lesser one, the energy that went into maintaining your limitation goes into expanding your awareness. Similarly, all the old energy that seemed to work against you or block your way now serves you by clearing your path and propelling you forward into greater growth.

So, alongside the limited belief of "I cannot have and do not deserve the goodness I want; everyone gets to have what they want but me," add something greater. Remember what you truly are: love. From that love, remember what you truly want. Then allow yourself that true wanting even though your personality tells you that you cannot have it. "Even though I feel that I cannot have and do not deserve it, I *want* the feeling of support in my life. *I am willing to receive support.*" "I *want* joy in my life even though I always thought it was meant for others rather than for me. I want joy anyway, and *I'm willing to have it.*"

When you do that, you are empowering yourself. None of your limitations is ever truly stopping you. The universe is generous, and you can always have what you deeply want. You just need to be willing. You will find that willingness as you open to true self.

As you move into this shift of awareness, the mental conditioning that had been holding you back may still continue speaking to you, saying things like, "You are not good enough." "You do not deserve to get what you want." "You cannot have it. If you get it you will just lose it again." Perhaps you also still have people around you who reflect that limited belief by remaining unsupportive of you. But now, even in the midst of that old limitation, you have greater choice. Without resisting that limitation, you can add a greater reality to it, one that empowers you: You can allow yourself to have.

When that old, unsupportive voice comes forward, you do not need to push it away. Simply acknowledge it. Say, "Here it is again." Then acknowledge and choose the new reality: "In spite of everything, I want what I want, and I'm willing to have it!" Align with the new voice, claim the deeper truth, and feel it in your body.

When you align this way daily, that new voice becomes as real to you as the old one—and, in time, even more real. Your attunement to truth deepens, and your overall experience of self grows to include having what you truly want. As this takes place, your outer life begins to shift and reflect that change.

Keep in mind that things do not change for you because you are a good person or because you are spiritual enough any more than because you dress well or hold good dinner parties. *It is your experience of self that determines what you create in your life.* When you allow yourself to remember your true self, feel your deepest desires, and receive goodness, so much more can come to you. Your life becomes richer.

ATTUNEMENT
Being Creator of Your Life #1

As you go about your life, stop for a moment several times a day to look at your life. Regardless of what you are doing, thinking, or feeling in the moment, say to yourself, "Yes, I have created this, and I love myself in this creation." Truly sink into the feeling of being the creator of your life, including the self-love. Doing this perhaps a minute ten to twelve times a day for a week will help bring a shift in your awareness and in your ability to be truly present with yourself in your life.

If you absolutely cannot go along with the "Yes, I have created this" part of the statement, focus on the "I love myself in this creation." That is the most important part.

When you say, "I love myself," sometimes you will feel it, and sometimes you won't; either way is all right. Sometimes self-love is noticeable alongside other feelings. Other times stronger feelings and physical sensations, like fear and frustration, may completely over shadow the feeling of self-love, which is a more subtle vibration. Self-love is there nonetheless, whether you feel it consciously or not.

If you do not feel the self-love, breathe. Look within as though you are looking for the most subtle colors of a sunset. If you find a subtle feeling of love, then breathe to acknowledge and receive it. If you do not notice any love, do not worry. It does not mean that the love is not there or that you are doing the exercise incorrectly. Your act of inner alignment has power whether or not you are able to feel it at the conscious level. It will be working at a deeper level you cannot yet feel and evidence will surface in time.

ATTUNEMENT
Being Creator of Your Life #2

For a week, take some time each day to scan your life. Recognize that you already have manifested a wealth of human experiences. Whether the feelings are pleasant or unpleasant does not matter. During the few minutes of scanning your life, you are being present with yourself and are noticing how much you already have created.

During this week, also consider allowing yourself to let go temporarily of the desire to change anything about your life that is not absolutely necessary. It can be liberating to take a week's vacation from feeling that anything is wrong and that you must do something about it.

This exercise may bring up the fear that you will be condoning everything in your life and will, therefore, be stuck with it as it is. Your mind may want to focus on change to avoid things as they are. But in spite of that reaction, see if you can allow yourself to take a vacation from trying, or even wanting, to change anything.

You may choose to balance the desire for change with a thought or affirmation such "I allow myself to receive learning and empowerment from everything I have created in my life" or "With self-love, I surrender to all I have created at this time, and I trust that it will guide me in growth." As always with affirmations, use wording that is simple and feels right for you.

The first lesson in being able to direct your manifesting powers more consciously is to allow what you already have done to be enough. As you stop running away from what you are living with right now, you begin to allow yourself to embrace your life as it is. You cannot accept yourself if you feel you must run away from what you already have created by quickly creating something better. Open your heart to the present, and learn from all that you have manifested. You are complete in this moment. You are an excellent manifestor already.

ATTUNEMENT
Being Creator of Your Life #3

Each night as you lie down to sleep, compassionately align with yourself as creator of your life. Feel your body relax as you think and feel the following: "I open to true wisdom and compassion in the heart of my being. I align with myself as creator and manifestor of my life. I allow this knowledge to become real to me." Adjust the wording to whatever feels most appropriate to you.

ATTUNEMENT
Being Creator of Your Life #4

1. Sit quietly for a few moments, and feel the gentle movement of your breath. . . . Allow your attention to drop into your heart. Feel your heart's openness and warmth, however subtle it may be.

2. Think or feel the following: "I align within the heart of my being, home of deep wisdom and compassion. . . . I call forth this wisdom and compassion to help me fully experience the life I already have created. . . . From my heart I align with myself as a creator and manifestor. . . . I am vibrant and aligned, always. . . ."

3. Sit for a few minutes in the reverberations of your affirmation. When you are ready to come out of your meditative state, breathe fully and become aware of your body. Then slowly open your eyes, stretch and move, and get up when you are ready.

LOUISA AND ABUNDANCE

"I sure need to experience the abundance of the universe," thought Louisa, "and fast."

Louisa was in a panic about money. Her boyfriend had just moved out, and he had been paying half the household bills for several years. Louisa's job was reliable and fulfilling, but she couldn't pay the hefty house payment by herself on the income it provided.

That night Louisa sat in quiet and meditated. As her breathing became gentler and more rhythmic, she softly intended for her awareness to go to "the place in my true self where I know that the universe is fully abundant and that I am a reflection of everything good in the universe."

As Louisa let her awareness drop within, she noticed the subtle well-being of true self circulating lightly within her. She let each breath go into that well-being, gently opening to the abundance she knew was there. Soon a tiny feeling of abundance began to emerge. With each breath, it became more real, calming and soothing her. It felt natural and right. With it came a knowing, without thoughts, that abundance was her core truth and that her life could mold itself to match that abundance. As Louisa ended the meditation, she made a commitment to herself to carry this knowing of abundance into her daily life.

The very next day, Louisa got two calls from people she didn't know, but who had heard of her, asking to hire her as a part time consultant for their businesses. Louisa hadn't done consulting in a decade! Yet here were two great offers. The hours fit easily around her regular job, the pay was a much higher hourly rate, and Louisa enjoyed the work. Taking those jobs gave Louisa the financial boost to cover her house payment and other expenses that popped up over the following years. Opening to true self abundance had become Louisa's foundation for manifesting and receiving the support she needed.

Part VI

ENLIVENED EMOTION

The Healing Power of Intense Feeling

32
Emotion as a Vehicle for Spirit

Emotion is the current of life force moving through the physical body and personality. To the degree we either resist or open to emotion, the personality resists or opens to life force—and therefore, unlimitedness—as it circulates through us. If emotion is restricted there is a loss of the joy of being human, which makes life seem oppressive and a struggle. If emotion is accepted and explored, felt and integrated in a balanced way, it creates a stronger connection within self as well as a deeper awareness of the interconnectedness of all people and all things.

Emotions are fluid. They have no set boundaries that keep them separate from each other. Any deeply felt emotion has the potential of opening the way for other emotions. For example, perhaps you have been so busy working on a project for several months that you haven't had a chance to be aware of your feelings. Then the project is completed, and you have time off. As your pace slows, you begin to feel emotions you did not realize were there.

Perhaps sadness is one of them. As you stay with your feelings, the sadness becomes a deep grief. You join a support group so you can have a safe place to feel and talk about your grieving. At some point as you move through the grief, you notice that a new joy begins to come into your life. You become aware that feeling your grief has cleared the space for the deeper joy to be felt also. The fluidity of emotion and your willingness to ride its current have guided you into a more vibrant intimacy with yourself.

It also is possible that the grief (or any other deeply felt emotion) may spontaneously make you aware of your connection to all other people who feel or have felt that emotion. Emotion is an energy that does not belong to anyone, does not begin or end within the person who feels it. Each emotion flows through all people, connecting them at the deepest level of physical awareness.

So, the grief you feel is not your grief; it is *the* grief that flows through all people. Similarly, the sadness or joy or love you feel is not yours, but is a universal energy you are tapping into and interpreting in your own way. As you open to this emotion in your life, it becomes a vibrant expression of your connection with self and others.

If you have a long-standing pattern of resisting emotion, you probably adopted that pattern in response to early environmental pressure. Perhaps your family upbringing, reinforced by experiences in society, taught you to resist, deny, or numb your feelings. If your present environment continues to reinforce your loss of emotional vitality rather than support you in reclaiming it, you may feel unable to change. Opening to deeply resisted or abandoned emotion can feel too threatening without compassionate, reliable outside support.

You do not have to open to emotion alone. In fact, you may not be able to do it alone. If it was a restrictive environment that caused you to close off to such an important aspect of your being, it may take an equally supportive environment, one with supportive people, to enable to you to open again. You deserve to reclaim your vibrant emotional self and, with it, the joy in life. You have every right to an environment of true support.

Finding that environment is the challenge. Seeking emotional support and not giving up if you have trouble finding it is itself important work. Sometimes people say, "I cannot find the right friends, the right therapist, the right group, the right technique," and so on. Maybe that has been true for you, too, up to this point, but how strong is your insistence? How committed are you? How demanding of life are you willing to be on your own behalf? How much are you willing to do to find or to create your supportive environment?

It may not always feel easy to find what you are seeking, but that does not mean it is not available. Whatever you truly long for is always possible. That is a given in life. How you get yourself to it, or how much you open yourself to receive, it is a mirror of your commitment to yourself and to reclaiming the brilliance of being fully alive.

Your emotions are sacred because they carry spirit.

Your personality includes your thoughts, emotions, and physical body as well as your relationship with the outer world and other people. It is the container you use to carry unlimited spirit as you move through the world. To the degree that you resist any part of that container, including your emotions, you restrict your ability to have fully conscious awareness of spirit. If you have aspirations to be highly spiritual, take loving care of your human self, for that is truly the divine work.

33
Love

As you came into this lifetime, you brought memory of the truth of your being. Unlimited spirit was still real to you, and you carried a capacity for love so complete that there was no separation; you were one with all things and all beings.

As we have already seen, you then became acculturated to the environment in which you grew up (your family, your schools, your social environment, and society in general) and took on the beliefs and experiences that surrounded you. This cultural consciousness was not based on unlimited being. In fact it told you that you were *not* one with others. Much of infancy and early childhood was spent learning that here in the physical world you are viewed and responded to as though you are completely separate. You were expected to conform to that reality of separation through your actions, your communication, and your inner experience. Through that perceived separation, your sense of self and your sense of all reality became limited.

That phase in your personality development was pivotal in your adaptation to physical reality and its limited consciousness. You came here to be in the physical world. You accepted the conditioning you received here and allowed it to affect your consciousness so you could explore physical reality more deeply.

Now, from the midst of your exploration of the separation and limitation of physical reality, you are starting to reopen to greater memory once more. This time you are inviting the awareness of true self slowly to become integrated into your personality, into the aspect of your being that has embodied the limited consciousness prevalent in the physical realm. At the core of this integration is the discovery that you no longer have to be restricted to choosing between submersion into the apparent limitation of physical reality or expansion into the freedom of unlimited being. It does not have to be either/or anymore. From the midst of any limited experience, you can open to unlimited true self.

You are developing the skill to contain and carry both
the limited and the unlimited together.

The integration of unlimited being into a reality previously based on limitation will ultimately be successful throughout the planetary culture. This success has already been destined, not by some powerful "outside" force or being, but by the collective consciousness of all beings involved. All beings bringing that destiny into reality, including you, have chosen their paths with care.

As you reclaim your deep memory of true self and unity with all things and all beings, you remember that this unity is based on unconditional love. People who are aligned in true self tap into a deep level from which they are flooded with unlimited love and the feeling of true Home. This deep love naturally radiates and connects them energetically and spiritually with all beings, physical and nonphysical.

All people desire this state of truth and love, whether or not they are conscious of it. Every person who feels a spiritual longing to go Home is longing for that state where nothing can interfere with the deep, unconditionally loving connection between self and others. What is so painful in the world is that there seem to be too many experiences that keep people from feeling their true connection with themselves and each other.

34
Hate

This is where hate comes in. At a basic level, hate is an outlet for the outrage at being separated from the deeply loving aspect of true self. Because of its intensity and extreme discomfort, hate then also becomes another of those separating experiences, adding further to a vicious cycle of disconnection from love. As hate blocks your deep, loving connection with self and others, the world seems more dangerous. More energy goes into defending and protecting yourself, which reinforces separation and takes you further away from conscious connection with true self.

For a moment, remember a situation when you hated another person. Your feeling in that situation may have been extreme rage and hatred, or it may simply have been hate in the form of low-grade anger or frustration that you could not seem to get over, the sort of chronic anger that quietly ate at you day after day.

Perhaps you thought your hate was due to something specific that person said or did. No matter what the hate seemed to be about, looking deeper into it probably would reveal that the event that inspired your hate brought up feelings that blocked your personality's awareness of your naturally loving, true self state. You lost contact with your true self's state of love in reaction to whatever the other person said or did. And because you lost connection with your true self, you then lost the ability to feel a deep level of unconditional love and connectedness to other people, particularly to the person you hated.

Remember, your most basic, true state is to be in unlimited love and connection with all beings. This unity brings a sense of inner peace and safety that is your greatest treasure. It is pure, unwavering well-being. When someone does something that stimulates a response within you that blocks your ability to feel loving connection, you feel cut off from your greatest well-being in a brutal way. Then not only do you feel hurt by what the person did, but you also suffer the injury of losing your connection to true self and unconditional love. That is heartbreaking.

Losing your natural ability to love
both yourself and the person who hurt you
is the greatest loss possible.

It is threatening when someone else's actions can take away your experience of true self and, therefore, unconditional love and your basic sense of peace, safety, and well-being in the world.

All hate is anguish at the loss of the ability
to feel loved and loving.

There is terror and outrage that someone has the power to cut you off from that love. If your true state of well-being can be taken away by what other people say and do, indeed, the world will seem brutal. It is difficult for the personality to rebalance itself when it feels unsafe.

Often the personality's response to this threat is to defend itself by positioning for battle—mentally, emotionally, physically. As you know, the cultural conditioning of physical reality tells you that when you are threatened, you make war. There are more wars happening in the world at this time than you can keep track of, and some are taking place in your own life.

Being at war does not necessarily mean that you attack in an outer way. You may simply carry on a long inner state of war, hating people for what they have done to you or taken from you. This may manifest as a list of things you believe to be wrong with them, things they shouldn't have done, ways they caused you or others pain, defects in their character, and so on.

Your list may be accurate; it may identify issues that do need to be worked out or that are good reasons for you not to socialize with those people. Yet more importantly, your most basic concern needs to be, "How can I release myself from this stance of war so I can reconnect with my true self? How can I reopen to the unlimited love that connects me with all life?"

One answer is to bring true self awareness back into your life whenever you are upset. Opening your awareness to your true self automatically brings back the unlimited love you have lost touch with. Doing this requires frequent use of your intention. It means choosing to add a more expanded awareness to whatever uncomfortable (and perhaps powerful) feelings you are having at the moment. Remember that you never have to stop your feelings, even if they seem limiting to you. You simply need to be creative about letting yourself extend beyond the limitations of those feelings to the subtle, unlimited love and well-being of true self.

Hatred is a very limiting emotion, giving you the sense of being closed off as though there is nothing that exists but that uncomfortable feeling. Your heart feels closed, and you are frustrated at not being able to loosen the grip your hatred has on you. Even when you think that hurting someone back or "teaching them a lesson" will make you feel better, those ideas appeal to you because unconsciously you assume that doing so will release you from the misery of hatred. (It won't.)

When you feel stuck in hating, you can use the discomfort to remind yourself of your desire to bring greater light into that aspect of your personality. You can pause for a moment and affirm, "Even in the midst of this distress, I choose to remember my true self and unlimited being. I open to the love that I am."

Sometimes the hate will be so powerful that there does not seem to be room for any other feeling. You may still need to deal with your anger and hate in constructive, practical terms, yet your affirmation will be laying the energetic circuitry for you to have a more expanded, true self experience, too.

Even one second of affirmation has a powerful effect, regardless of whether you feel it in the moment. The greatest effect takes place at a level deeper than feeling. So if you repeat your affirmation sincerely even a hundred times over a period of days or weeks without feeling the connection, there will still be an accumulative effect of all those seconds. At some point your inner circuitry will become strong enough that you will begin to notice a difference.

Sooner or later you will notice that even in the midst of hating there can still be the experience of true self and unconditional love. You will begin to stay open to love even when you feel hate. Then hate will no longer limit you; it will no longer separate you from love and expanded awareness. Hate will no longer be a dangerous, destructive feeling that must be avoided or denied; it will be just another human feeling through which the light of truth can shine and bring transformation.

What a glorious breakthrough! At that point you will be able to hold more than one reality in your consciousness at a time. Do not undervalue this ability; it is the secret to expanding your consciousness and opening to new possibilities. For this reason, it is a recurring theme throughout this book.

The ability to hold more than one reality
in your consciousness at the same time
frees you from limitation.

Even when you feel angry, sad, frustrated, or hateful, you can simultaneously feel your unlimited spirit. It is like a ray of light shining into the darkness. As you continue to open to unlimited spirit, the ray of light grows. Yet even if the darkness of hate closes your heart and seems bigger than that single ray of light, the ray of light has greater power because it comes from true self.

When you are able to contain both the light and the dark together, that is an enlightening state. It means that you no longer have to choose one experience over another. You do not have to choose love *or* hate, blame *or* forgiveness, sadness *or* joy, anger *or* openheartedness. You are no longer polarized; no particular feeling boxes you in and keeps you from the light of true self. You then have access to the full range of human experiences you came into this life to embrace.

35

Forgiveness

Forgiveness is the antidote for hate; it is the path back to true self. The best suggestion for finding forgiveness in your heart for someone you hate is to find forgiveness for yourself first. If you are feeling resentment or hate, no matter how much it is justified, you are suffering and need self-forgiveness. Self-forgiveness releases suffering and restores balance.

Frequently people do not want to focus on forgiving themselves because they think it means they have to admit guilt for something. They think forgiveness is given only to someone who has done something wrong. It is important to realize that people often need forgiveness even when they have done nothing wrong.

Forgiving is giving forth compassion.

Rather than seeing forgiveness as blaming yourself or excusing someone else for wrongdoing, see it as simply extending compassion where compassion is needed. Then it becomes easier to forgive everyone, including yourself.

Even if you believe someone else has wronged or hurt you, forgiving that person (or coming to peace with the situation) may be easier if you extend a hand of true compassion to yourself first. "I forgive myself. In the face of everything this person has done or has put me through, I extend loving compassion to myself. I forgive myself for the pain and anger I have felt."

There is nothing wrong with your pain and anger, yet forgiving yourself for feeling it may still be important. Intense pain or anger is often accompanied by an automatic sense of guilt or shame, so it can help to realize that beneath your pain, anger, or hatred you may have hidden guilt or shame about those feelings. Because that guilt or shame adds more discomfort, you may unconsciously avoid the whole set of feelings by becoming self-righteous: "Well, they wronged me, so they deserve to have something bad happen to them." "He should come and apologize to me first." "I would never do the kind of thing she did!"

Whenever you are at war with someone else,
you are always at war with yourself, too.

The deep guilt or shame about your feelings is your war against yourself. When you are self-righteous with someone else to avoid feeling your own guilt or shame, you are fighting yourself as much as you are fighting the other person. You have probably already discovered that such a dual battle becomes all consuming and self-destructive—a war you can never win.

In the midst of this complex web of intense and difficult emotion, how do you create healing so you can move on? Simply forgiving yourself cuts through everything and returns you to a state of empowerment and simplicity. "I forgive myself for feeling hurt. I forgive myself for anger and hatred. I forgive myself for separating from the true heart of my being."

Or, because forgiving is to give forth compassion, you may feel more comfortable with different wording: "I give myself compassion in the midst of this pain. I give myself compassion in the midst of my anger or hatred. I give myself compassion for having been separated so easily from my true self by what someone else said or did."

Truly giving yourself compassion—not self-righteousness for how you have been wronged or self-pity for how terrible the ordeal has been, but genuine, glowing compassion—softens everything. With that softening, your battle armor begins to melt; your war stance becomes less rigid because you are gaining a truer power. As you continue feeling compassion for yourself, the war stance will soften even more. It will happen gently and naturally as you are ready to move into your greater strength.

So it is a matter of extending, from the midst of that position of war, a hand of compassion to self. "Yes, I feel the pain, and I give compassion to myself in the midst of it. Even though it may feel impossible at this moment, I want to be open to my unlimited self-love. I want to reclaim the love that streams through my being and unites me with all other beings in peace and truth."

Keep in mind that all current experiences of hate carry a hidden registry of previous, formative experiences when you felt forced into similarly devastating separation from true self. You never experience hate that is truly only of the moment. All hate carries the memory and burden of unresolved outrage at having lost your conscious experience of true self in the past. So, a current conflict that brings you to unbearable rage or hatred may be an excellent opportunity to begin deeper healing of your past.

When you find yourself automatically in a war stance from which you feel unable to release either yourself or the person you hate, pay close attention. You may notice that your feelings of hate seem to go beyond the current situation, trailing into your past so deeply that you no longer have clear images or memories to go with the feelings. As you extend compassion to yourself and your armor softens, earlier experiences of being separated from true self may come forward to be recognized. Perhaps even your initial experience of separation from true self will reveal itself for healing.

> *Remember that your hate need not close you down;*
> *it can remind you of compassion and give you the*
> *opportunity to heal some powerful feelings.*

Your way through the unbearable pain of hating is to know that, more than anything, you want to regain your experience of true self and unlimited being. You want true self even more than you want revenge, even more than you want your "enemies" to finally see how wrong, bad, or flawed they have been. Your desire for the unlimited love, peace, and divinity you truly are becomes most important. This alignment of priorities brings you to a position of power; your energies are directed with true purpose.

You may find that your energy system is not quite strong enough to hold that alignment of priorities for very long at a time. That's all right.

Frequency matters more than sustainability. The more frequently you choose true self, even for periods as brief as a few seconds, the more often your energy system adjusts and strengthens itself. Then, over time, it becomes easier to maintain the true self experience for longer periods.

If you have lived decades with a habit of going into war posture when you are threatened, your energy pattern is well developed to support your being at war. It may take time for your energy system to restructure itself to the pattern of compassion and forgiveness. In that period of transition, which could be days, weeks, months, or even years, be patient with yourself. The time it takes your system to restructure will ultimately enable you to hold the experience of true self and unlimited being more continuously in your daily life.

Be aware that your personality may periodically object to this focus on forgiveness and reconnection with true self. The personality has been conditioned to self-righteousness or self-pity so it may still insist that other people be made to see what they did wrong, or be punished, or be shamed, or be made to apologize, and so on. There is no need to silence your personality; it is an expression of your consciousness and is, therefore, worthy of being heard. But you may want to remember that your personality's greatest skill is not in bringing you Home to greater truth and inner connection.

Perhaps you are used to thinking of your personality as your ego. *Ego* is a more commonly used term than *personality*, yet for our purposes they are the same and can be used interchangeably. We can frame it both ways.

Because of the various psychological and spiritual usages of the term *ego*, you may tend to think of your ego as a problem, maybe a self-centeredness or something you must overcome if you want to attain spiritual enlightenment. Let's not frame ego that way. For our purposes, ego is simply the part of your mind that adapted long ago to losing your connection to true self. It became the leader in that state of loss and has been responsible for your survival in limited reality.

Everything your ego thinks and perceives is in the context of separation and limitation. To your ego, true self is not real. Therefore, desires and actions that come from your ego never fully take into account that unity and unlimited love are possible. In short, your ego can tell you how to operate in a limited world *without* your connection to true self; it cannot show you how to reconnect. For that you must extend beyond your ego and invite your true self to show you the way. Forgiving yourself in the midst of hate is a powerful invitation.

So you see, forgiveness begins primarily in your relationship with yourself. Empowering yourself with the gifts of your own heart frees you of injuries it seems others have caused you. As you receive your own forgiveness, or compassion, forgiving others happens naturally as a side effect of your own healing.

MEDITATION
Forgiveness

1. Close your eyes, and breathe easily and fully. As you breathe, let each breath fill you with a feeling or image of love, even if it is very subtle. Enjoy the love, and allow it to grow within you.

2. When you are ready, think of someone whom you have difficulty forgiving. Imagine this person coming forward and facing you at a safe distance. Let yourself feel how uncomfortable it feels to hold feelings of blame, hate, frustration, or resentment toward this person.

3. As you face this person, make only the following change in the situation: Breathe love into yourself again. This love is not necessarily for the other person: It is for you. You are being filled with the light of love, the feeling of love, the thought of love. . . . Each breath gives you more love for yourself, even as you remain in the presence of the other person.

4. From this presence with love, think or speak phrases like the following: "I give love and compassion to myself right now." "I allow my true self to fill me with its light." "I forgive myself for my pain and suffering. I allow myself to be healed by love."

5.   Feel the meaning of your words take effect as you think or speak them. Stay with feelings of love, compassion, forgiveness, and healing for as long as you like.

6.   Now imagine that the other person fades, disappears, or walks out of your image. . . . When you are ready to come out of this meditation, your compassion for yourself comes with you into the world. As you open your eyes, the love and healing remain; they are truly within you now.

36
Anger

Your exploration of love will at some point bring you to anger's door. No matter how many techniques you learn for loving yourself and others, sooner or later you must make your peace with anger. Your challenge is to learn to find your way of receiving the glorious light of life even when you are angry.

There is nothing wrong with being angry. Anger can alert you that something inappropriate or threatening (from your personality's perspective) is happening in a situation and can mobilize your energy to take constructive action. Yet because anger is usually expressed in distorted and destructive ways, and because anger often activates the personality and blocks awareness of the unconditionally loving self, many people feel that anger is not a "spiritual" experience.

Understand that spirit is in every thought and feeling you can have. Spirit is in every cell of your body and every aspect of your personality. You can never be truly separate from spirit because you and everything about you, including anger, *are* spirit. So, every experience, including anger, is spiritual and serves a high purpose.

At the personality level, it is important for you to deal with the specific issues that trigger your anger. Sometimes this will mean standing up for yourself in a conflict or a threatening situation. Other times you may need to assess whether your anger is really related to the situation that triggered it or is an old emotional pattern that no longer serves you. If you have trouble knowing how to take appropriate action with your anger (or with your response to someone else's), by all means get assistance from a wise and reliable source. There are excellent books as well as skilled therapists available to help you develop a healthy relationship with anger. It is worth pursuing and is part of the life-long ritual of honoring and clearing your personality so it can serve you on your path of growth.

For now, let's leave the psychological aspects of anger as well as its appropriate expression. (These may need to be explored in circumstances that give you the ongoing support you need.) Instead, let's focus on the energetic aspect of anger and how you can open to the vitality it carries.

The vitality of life force is within all emotion;
this vitality is your birthright.

When you allow yourself to have the vitality within your anger, you will find it easier to allow yourself to have everything else you truly want in life. It all comes down to allowing life force to flow through you.

Because life force is the basic energy flow of life, it is what connects you to physical reality, literally giving you life and enabling you to be present and active in the physical world. Holding back or stopping your life force would be foolish, ludicrous! Why would you want to stop the flow of energy that gives you vitality and sustains your physical existence? Yet, when your anger is denied, your vitality also is denied. If you do not let your anger through in a clean, open, life-affirming way, it works against you, separating you energetically from the world you came here to embrace.

This does not mean that to allow yourself vitality you must always be angry. Vitality is experienced in all emotions and states of being. You have a wide repertoire! But by denying or withholding your anger you deny yourself part of your basic connection with life.

If anger seems negative to you,
you are probably thinking of distorted anger.

Anger in its pure form is not rageful, dangerous, or violent. It is not pent up, misdirected, or discharged in emotional attack. Pure anger is a feeling that creates a conduit for energy and flushes the life force through your system. It is an extending energy, connecting people rather than separating them, prompting communication rather than isolation or conflict. Pure anger can be as powerful as love or joy in opening your heart and healing your body, and restoring healthy connection between you and others.

Why, then, is anger so often experienced as negative and destructive?

We live in a culture where the personality perceives itself as separate from true self and unconditional well-being. To compensate, it relies heavily on the ability to be "in control" and trusts emotions only to the extent it can remain in control of them. This need for control prevents us from trusting emotions that convey life force powerfully and are harder to control.

Because the personality is unaware that we all are truly one with life force, life force seems separate from us and bigger than we are. So the power of life force, which we cannot control, is perceived as a threat to whatever control we may have established in life. Emotions, such as anger, that are naturally strong conductors of life force are feared and generally are not well managed.

As a culture we have worked so hard at controlling anger that often we mistake even the faintest feeling of anger—ours or other people's—for the need to have greater control, and we react at that level. So, either expressing our anger or facing other people's anger can easily turn into a battle where we try to control others or to keep from being controlled by them. We may fling our anger at people through a litany of complaints or subtle manipulation in an attempt to control them, the situation, or our vulnerability—instead of allowing our anger to show us how much we want well-being and connection.

Perhaps that is what you do, or perhaps you keep your anger bottled up to ensure you don't use it destructively. When you resist or disallow anger, that energy doesn't go away; it's an alive, moving force. Because it must go somewhere, it often is rerouted into a less clear and less direct expression. The energy of disowned anger can be turned inward and unconsciously used against yourself. Fatigue, illness, depression, hopelessness, insecurity, and emotional defensiveness are some of the possible results.

You may have unknowingly adopted such a self-destructive emotional pattern early in life. Perhaps in your family no one tolerated being the recipient of your anger, so you learned not to express it to others. It may have been acceptable, however, for you to turn your anger against yourself through self-criticism or self-hatred. You may even have gotten the message that if you were angry at someone, you actually deserved to have something bad happen to you because of it. This conditioning could have set the pattern for the energy of your anger to come back to you in destructive ways.

Considering the narrow range of options the culture offers, it is natural that you may resist your anger as well as the anger of others. The irony is that in the fight to maintain control, you have forgotten anger's real purpose! You have forgotten that anger is a energy of communication and connection rather than of alienation and opposition. You have forgotten that anger is a powerful feeling that triggers your energy system to open more fully to life force. You have forgotten that being open to the flow of life force as it streams through your body and *opens you to true self* is what life is all about and is, therefore, more important than "winning" any battle.

As you develop the ability to receive the pure,
vital energy within anger,
you open to a powerful new healing source.

As the energy of creation, vital life force is the most profound healing energy there is. So in its pure form, anger is a healing energy rather than a destructive one. Because few people have learned to be open to and accepting of undistorted anger, few people realize the tremendous healing power it carries.

Exploring this element of anger requires that you hold a clear focus and pay attention. You need a strong, conscious commitment to self to stay present and follow through on the progression of feelings and experiences that will emerge. As you open to the pure vitality of life in anger, you will find yourself beginning to open to pure experience at many other levels as well. Vitality links you to true self, and the effects of that connection are always far-reaching.

A primary step in opening to the vitality of anger is to notice that when you are angry, you have tremendous energy at your disposal and you have choice about how you direct it. You can use that energy to dam yourself up inside, deaden yourself, hold yourself back, think abusive thoughts about yourself, or send it out toward other people in similarly destructive ways. Or, you can receive the gift of vitality that comes with that emotion and be enlivened by it. That vitality then nourishes you, enriching your life and your relationships with other people.

Anger is an emotion and a physiological response in the body. Whether you use the emotion in a destructive way or a life-affirming way directly affects the chemistry of your body, which in turn enhances or diminishes your physical, mental, emotional, and energetic well-being. Your choice in interpreting and directing the energy of anger is what makes all the difference. If this choice is not made consciously, it happens unconsciously from your long held patterns of habit. Whichever way it occurs, your choice determines whether you move into increased experiences of vibrant life or into depletion.

Underneath anger is usually a feeling of helplessness.

Even if you are not consciously in touch with it, that helplessness may cause you to overlook the true power you always have in anger: the power to choose life. You probably are not trained to recognize such power. Few parents say to their angry children, "You are angry. It's a strong feeling, and I want you to notice how much power you have. You have a choice to use this power in a life-affirming way. How can you do that? What would be a good way? Talk to me about it, and I will help you." If you did not get this support from a parent, you can learn to give it to yourself.

When you feel angry, stop briefly and take a few deep breaths to become present with yourself. Consciously notice that, in spite of any distressing emotion that may be circulating through your system, you are at a point of power. You have the power of choice.

As you focus on this thought, you may discover some resistance to claiming your power when you are angry. Your habituated reaction to anger may seem to have a life of its own and may be difficult to stop, even for just a moment. As impractical and uncomfortable as it may be, unconsciously you may also be attached to the familiarity of your old pattern. Watch for your resistance. It is natural. Notice it and then ask yourself, "Do I want to go with the resistance this time and keep the old pattern, or do I want to make a change and remember that I am at a point of power here?"

Of course, the power is not power over the person or situation that is the focus for your upset feelings. It is the power of being able to choose how much affirmation of life you will carry in your body. That is far more important than any issue you are likely to be angry about.

Because the cultural patterning of anger is so strong,
it is easy to get stuck arguing the issues
and trying to gain and maintain control.

Imagine, for example, that you are in an argument with someone and your temper flares. You are tempted to fall into your old pattern of using your anger to intimidate, belittle, or find fault with your adversary to win the argument and, therefore, avoid the feeling of being defeated yourself. Or perhaps your tendency is to pretend you are not angry, to sulk, or to make the other person feel guilty so they will retreat. In these cases, the pure energy of your anger is misdirected, which short-circuits your flow of vitality. In this compromised state, you have literally forgotten your source of true well-being, and this is a very real loss to you. Is gaining control in an argument worth the cost of diminished vitality to your own system?

Learning to give anger its natural, direct expression, which includes giving up control over others, allows the pure vitality of anger to stream through all levels of your being, nourishing and revitalizing every cell in your body. This in itself is one definition of "winning" in an argument. For example, if the other person's opinion or decision prevails, you can have the personal victory of walking away with vibrant life that is not dependent on the outcome of the argument.

This certainly does not mean you must always make an either/or choice between inner, personal victory and outer effectiveness. You need not retreat or be passive in a conflict to maintain your energetic integrity. In fact, staying open to life force can increase your ability to be centered and empowered within yourself, to hold your ground, and to communicate with the strength or passion you feel.

What you may need to do, however, is start noticing your misdirection of anger as it happens and then give yourself some new options. Learning new techniques for healthy containment and expression of anger can help tremendously. Also, choosing vitality often in your life and becoming familiar with what it feels like in a variety of situations can establish a recognizable base of well-being, which you can return to when you become angry.

The bottom line is that sometimes your expression of anger will get you the outer results you want and sometimes it will not. Yet, all experience has one basic purpose: to bathe you with unlimited life. When you accept this truth, revitalizing yourself by being fully open to receiving life force becomes your highest priority. You can then choose your response to every situation based on what would enhance your flow of true vitality and well-being rather than diminish it.

As you live with this clear, aligned intention, other people's ways of dealing with anger may become less relevant as models for your own behavior. You are unplugging from the culturally held consciousness about anger. While the cultural beliefs still include the unconscious assumption that anger equals an inner loss or death, you are beginning to use anger as a vehicle for vibrant life.

At the moment when they are at a point of power,
most people have no idea of the magnificent choice they face.

Given conscious choice, most people would choose increased vibrancy; yet relatively few actually realize that their anger can take them there. Without a greater awareness, cultural habit prevails and people tend to let anger restrict their flow of vibrant life force. The body and energy system know the difference between being life enhanced or life deprived; even subtle restriction of the life force is recognized as depletion. Some people react to anger as though it threatens their survival. Ironically, it is the act of restricting their flow of life force in reaction to anger that is the true threat. Without understanding this dynamic, people respond to anger, their own as well as other people's, with fear.

Unplugging from this cultural pattern means a profound change in your life; again it is natural that your personality may display resistance. If that happens, it may help to stop, take a deep breath, and then briefly lend a compassionate ear to the resistance. Hear what the voice of resistance has to say, and take notes for it. Write a few words, perhaps even two or three sentences, to capture the message. This allows the resistance to be expressed and then released onto paper.

If the resistance returns, gently repeat the procedure as needed. Important information about your inner process and your personality's needs may be revealed to you in this way. By expressing, hearing, and releasing the resistance, you are redirecting its flow. It no longer operates in a closed circuit, keeping you stuck. It is being trained to inform you and then pass through, leaving you free to make new choices.

Remember, resistance to empowering change comes from the aspect of the personality that does not yet know you can have more fulfillment than you have had in the past. It operates from habit and limitation and tries to protect you.

As a creation of your unlimited spirit, your personality
is worthy of being loved and honored;
you just don't have to believe it as you once did.

Honor your personality by hearing its concerns; then take another deep breath and go back to your point of power. Feel your anger and consider your choice consciously. "I feel a powerful energy moving through me. I can choose to let it enliven me or shut me down. Vitality or deadness. Vibrant life or slow depletion. Which do I choose?"

When you are at this point of considering aliveness or depletion, it may sometimes feel impossible to choose aliveness. The old conditioning may still be too strong. Your inner self-critic may interpret this as a sign of personal failure on your part. It may say that you are a weak person, that you are not enlightened enough, that you do not deserve to feel good, or something equally deflating. The content of these critical messages is usually not true and does not matter anyway. What is more helpful than evaluating your self-worth is simply being honest with yourself about when you are choosing aliveness and when you are choosing depletion.

When you choose depletion, you are not making a bad choice. You are simply doing what you are doing. You can still accept yourself. In fact, you can still full-heartedly love yourself, even though you may wish you could have made a different choice. Noticing with conscious awareness which choice you are making while giving yourself acceptance, support, and love in that moment is in itself significant empowerment.

The good news is that you are all right regardless of the choice you make. There are no good choices or bad choices in life. There are ones that bring you into empowering experience of vital life force and choices that diminish that experience, but there is no good and bad. All the choices you make are done with unlimited blessing from unlimited beings. And in all those choices, absolute love and life force are still the core of who you truly are, regardless of what you experience in the moment when you take your action.

There is nothing wrong with you when you make a choice that restricts the flow of vitality through your being. In fact, giving yourself acceptance and love in that situation nourishes your system and lays new circuitry that will enable you to make a more life-affirming decision the next time, or the next, or the next. If you catch yourself being unable to direct your anger in a new, life-affirming way, then breathe, remember the love that you are, and pat yourself on the back for being an excellent human being who is pursuing the exploration of limitation.

If you believe that anger is destructive, it may be difficult to allow yourself to open to it, even though you know that anger carries vital healing force. Be very patient, gentle, and loving with yourself and take the process slowly. If you are at risk of being overwhelmed, or have reason to fear your patterns of anger, or need new input to develop healthy expressions for this powerful emotion, support yourself by getting qualified outside help.

Anger is not always comfortable, but it is far more comfortable when it is allowed to move through as the vitality of life rather than resisted as something negative or dangerous. Anger is dangerous if you use it against yourself or others, but that is not its real purpose. It is not meant to be a weapon. Anger can be a healing force when its energy is allowed to flow through freely—and even gently—as a way to connect you with Source.

When you can allow yourself to feel anger in a way that does not close you off to yourself or others, but instead opens you to the life force that feeds and nurtures you, you will not fear anger so much. In opening to the vitality of life within anger, you are opening to true self while becoming more present in your physical body. You are bringing the truth of your spirit into physical experience, which is the essential purpose of your journey into form.

ATTUNEMENT
Staying Aware in Anger

You are setting new patterns, which require repetition. New experience has to be real to the body before the automatic emotional responses can genuinely change. During the time of repatterning, staying conscious and witnessing your choices will help. When anger surfaces, you can go through the following steps:

1. Feel the vibrant energy.

2. Recognize that you are at a point of power.

3. Notice that you have a choice to enhance or restrict your flow of life force.

4. Become clear on what constructive action will best support your well-being and vibrant aliveness.

5. Stay aware as you take whatever constructive action you choose.

6. Give yourself acceptance and notice how it feels.

MEDITATION
Healing Through Anger

The following meditation can give you practice in shifting your patterns of energetic response to anger. You can experiment with it in small increments of perhaps five to fifteen minutes every few days or weeks. It is best to choose times when you are not feeling strong or overwhelming anger, so you have some range within which to maneuver. Do not move so far into anger that you lose control. You need to be able to guide yourself in and out of the anger gently. Consider having someone else with you to support or guide you until you're comfortable doing it yourself.

(Note: If while doing this visualization you sense that your feelings of anger may become too uncomfortable or intense, simply stop. Open your eyes, breathe gently and easily for a few moments, and bathe yourself in love. Give yourself compassion for having gone as far as you were ready to go. Honor your limits and do not push yourself. Move into an activity that balances and nourishes you., or talk with a support person.)

1. Begin by imagining a situation when you were angry. You may remember a real-life situation, or you may make one up. Give yourself a few moments to let the situation form in your imagination.... Let yourself feel some of the anger—not enough to overwhelm you, but just enough to remember how anger feels....

2. Also imagine that your purpose right now is not to change the situation that makes you angry or to change anyone else's mind or actions. Instead, your purpose is simply to allow the vitality of life to flow through your body and your energy system along with the anger. Vitality is the main experience, and the anger is just the medium for it. Gently allow your energy system to open so vitality streams through you....

3. You can feel the anger, yet you don't have to put it into action or words. You don't have to fight. You don't have to convince or interact with anyone. In this moment, you are simply in that situation to experience the nurturing flow of vitality that anger carries.

4. There is plenty of space for the vitality to move through your system. This energy, or life force, has a natural wisdom of its own. As it flows, it feeds and nourishes every cell in your body. It brings life and radiance into your being. Absorb and accept this healing force.

5. Now imagine that the angry situation you were facing disappears into light. All stress disappears with it. The light lingers long enough to cleanse you of any residue of anger, conflict, frustration, or discomfort, leaving you washed with radiant vitality and well-being.

6. When you are ready to come out of your meditative state, breathe fully and become aware of your body. Then slowly open your eyes, stretch and move, and get up when you are ready.

ATTUNEMENT
Healing Through Anger: Short Version

After you feel familiar with the meditation and are comfortable guiding yourself through it, the next step is to open consciously to this process while you are already feeling anger. It can be done in a minute or two—or even a few breaths. Start in a situation involving a very low, easily manageable level of anger. As you are successful, you can slowly work up to more challenging situations.

If you find that this exercise increases your anger rather than soothes or balances it, stop the exercise and turn to a self-soothing process that is more effective and constructive for you. To practice using the vitality in anger in a healing way, the anger cannot be so strong as to overwhelm you.

1.   Pause for a moment and take a few deep, easy breaths. With those breaths turn your awareness to the gentle vitality in anger.

2.   Allow the vitality to flow through your system in a natural, gentle way. It does not escalate your anger, but soothes or balances it. Let yourself feel this positive life force flowing through your body and nourishing your cells and tissues.

3.   Know that you are experiencing a healing energy that can show you how to constructive deal with the situation.

4.   As you close this exercise, take three gentle breaths while imagining that the love that you are is radiating through you.

CLARK

Clark swaggered into my office. He was thirty-something, tall, broad shouldered, and muscular in a way that says, "Yeah, I work out. A lot." Clean cut, good looking, and confident, he was a guy's guy; I could picture him chopping wood. His face looked open, like it had no secrets. We said our Hello's, smiled, and shook hands, but I was on alert. It wasn't fear, just the visceral wake-up I get when instinct tells me, "No matter how convincing this individual's persona looks, there's something different underneath."

As our session started Clark told me he was there because his girlfriend, a client of mine, thought it might help their relationship. She thought he had problems with emotional intimacy. He went on to say that he agreed. He didn't know why, but whenever he started to get close to a woman he would pull away. He really loved this girlfriend and felt drawn to build a future with her, but whenever he thought about it he would get confused and then say or do things that created distance between them. He wondered if he ever was going to be capable of settling down and enjoying a committed relationship. As I asked questions it became clear that he didn't think he had any fears; his only problem was that this mystifying dynamic kept occurring.

Our conversation turned to his work as a police officer. He talked easily about the challenges of the job and his commitment to serving his community. He went on to tell me about his camaraderie with his fellow officers, the importance of keeping emotions in check, and the necessity of reacting to situations according to procedure. As he described some of the dangerous situations he took in stride daily, I said, "That sounds pretty scary." "No," he replied, "I don't really feel scared."

When we talked about how violent and irrational some of the people he had arrested had been, his easy going manner disappeared, and his tone quickly became reproachful. These were terrible, awful people who deserved whatever punishment they got, was his opinion. "All of them?" I wondered. Yes, pretty much, he was certain.

He began a story he was sure would convince me. In the middle of the night, seven or eight years previously, he and his partner had been trying to arrest an out-of-control, violent man who had been threatening people on the street. Soon into the story, Clark couldn't find words bad enough (that he was willing to say in front of me) to describe the man. "This guy was the worst of the worst, scum of the earth. People like him are hardly human," was his sentiment.

"We were trying to cuff him, but he was too violent to catch and hold. He was high on something. He felt no pain, and there was no reasoning with him." Clark paused to inhale. "That son-of-a-bitch had a knife. My partner turned away for a split second, *just a split second*, to open the car door, and that #*+&*!! charged at him."

Words poured out of him now. "My partner didn't have a chance, it all happened too fast. The guy was going to stab him; he was going to *kill* him. I had no choice. I HAD to save my partner! I pulled the trigger. I shot that slimy, no-good #*+&*!! He went down instantly."

Clark's face crumbled. He stared at me dumbfounded as he continued, "I'd shot him in the stomach, and his blood was all over the sidewalk. We called for an ambulance and tried to stop the bleeding while we waited, but"—sobs were starting to break free—"it was no use, that bastard died within minutes."

Clark's face was in his hands now as the weight he had been carrying pressed on him. Sobs shook his shoulders, freeing the grief and torment he had kept strapped down all those years so it wouldn't reach his heart and make him feel. When the flood of feelings came, Clark didn't resist.

"I hated that guy, but I still didn't want to kill him." His face lifted, eyes wide. "Underneath, he was still a person. I killed a person. A real person! I wanted to be someone who helped, not killed."

His grief gushed out now in a free release of tears. There was no hiding and no holding back. No keeping the feelings at bay. No more strapping down anything to keep it still and silent. Clark's eyes stayed with mine as tears and words flowed.

"I had to protect my partner, but I didn't want to kill anybody. I never wanted to kill anybody." As Clark talked on, his body softened, his shoulders dropped, bravado was gone.

"Is it possible you're feeling grief?" I asked. He nodded, but seemed mystified, not quite sure how he had gotten there.

"Is it possible that after you shot that man, and he died, what disturbed you most was not how horrible a person he had been, but how horrible your grief felt?"

"Yes..." Clark's words emerged slowly, his voice low, "I had no idea, no idea. Grief for that man, for the life he lost." He looked at me with surprise, "And grief for myself. I lost something that night. My heart has been broken ever since."

I asked Clark to close his eyes and let his awareness settle gently in his heart. When he nodded he was there, I continued guiding him deeper, into his true self, into that aspect of his being that is so all-loving and all-nurturing that it is not afraid of broken hearts, or shootings, or grief that feels too big. Clark breathed into his true self and sighed. Big sighs, sighs that had waited at the outskirts of anger and judgment seven or eight years to be signaled that it was safe now and they were welcome. Sighs and tears mingled. Then peace settled in.

When Clark opened his eyes, he looked at me with calm. The current of emotion had carried him Home, to true self, to his ever present source of comfort and compassion, to gentle shores. With new self-compassion, Clark talked more about the incident, how it had affected him, and how little encouragement he had gotten at his job to show his pain. Noticeably absent from the rest of our conversation was any more judgment or disgust about the difficult and dangerous "bad guys" so plentiful in his work. It wasn't necessary anymore.

No wonder Clark had had trouble being emotionally intimate with his girlfriend; he had put up a barrier to emotional intimacy with himself. To keep his grief at bay he had had to keep himself out of his own heart. His source of deepest love, vulnerability, and connection to people, to *all* people—girlfriends and bad guys and everyone in between—had been off limits. He had kept to the outer periphery of that barrier, where, like at the edge of a solar system, conditions that nourish humans are absent.

We often forget that our primary, human relationship is not with our romantic partner; it's with our self. The more intimately present we are with ourselves, the more intimate we can be with others. Connecting with true self is the deepest intimacy we can have. Emotion, even anger and judgment, can take us there.

Expressing our emotions in a safe environment—whether telling our story to a caring, compassionate person, writing in our journal, or simply speaking out loud kindly to ourselves when we're alone—can carry us to true self if that is where we want to go. True self is big enough to cradle all our feelings, all our stories, all our fears that life might be too much for us. True self is the source of the love and compassion we have in our hearts, and the safety we need to live there.

Part VII

MY STORY CONTINUES

Painting

37
Breakthrough

In 1999 I was struck by a sudden and all consuming desire to paint. Certain for the previous 30 years that I was not a painter and could never be one because I couldn't paint the way we had been taught in high school art class, I was intimidated by my new desire. Just walking into an art supply store made me sweat. I was sure the people working there could see that I had never held a canvas, was in awe of the word "palette", and didn't even know how to squirt paint from a tube. I felt marked as an outsider, someone who didn't belong in the world of art.

Scared as I was, I took a three-day, outdoor painting workshop. The only novice in the group, I was mostly ignored while the instructor helped her more advanced students. When I got stuck I had to wait an hour or two to get her help, so I stopped asking. Being left to flail around by myself turned out to be a blessing because it was *my* flailing. Without instruction about such things as perspective, light, shadow, and composition, there was no "right" way of painting to limit me, and I experimented freely.

To my surprise I fell profoundly in love with the acrylic paint (which I *was* able to squeeze from the tube after all!). The blobs of thick, wet colors were like little worlds on my palette, momentarily still before swooshing across the universe of my canvas, colliding and combining into creations I wouldn't have known how to plan. Applying the paint was luscious, sensuous, and exciting in a way that I had never known creative expression could be.

Ecstasy happened on the third day. As I painted, joy streamed through my body with such intensity that the bottoms of my feet felt on fire. Oddly, I didn't mind; it was a glorious kind of pain. But every hour or two, the buildup of vibrancy in my body became too uncomfortable to contain, so I had to stop painting and jump up and down a few times to release some of the energy.

38

Integrating

After the workshop, I turned my extra bedroom into a painting studio. Immersed in painting every day, I thought of and talked about little else. My true self coaching and classes, which I loved unwaveringly, continued, but other practicalities of life seemed distant, of minimal importance. Errands went undone, and I stuffed bills into a desk drawer with a weak promise to revisit them "later."

Yet one errand I performed enthusiastically was buying my painting supplies. The very art store that used to make me sweat and feel inadequate now made me as happy as a toy store does a child. Now I felt at home there. It was my "Cheers"—I was a regular, and everybody greeted me by name. The owner, Mike, liked to tease me as we carried armloads of canvases to my car and then went back for the bags of paint, "Next time, just back a truck up to the door!"

After five months of immersion in creative bliss, I surfaced enough to realize that I had spent $3,000 to create my studio and keep it stocked with materials I voraciously used, and that I was getting second Overdue notices for bills still waiting in the drawer. Wonderful as painting was for me, I felt like an addict with a habit I couldn't afford.

Giving up painting was inconceivable, so it was time to start selling my work. Having no idea how artists did that, I packed 17 of my biggest paintings into the car and took them to an art gallery in town. The two owners, Deanna and Dayla, were kind and gracious women who gently explained that artists usually submit photos rather than hauling in all their goods, but they chose five paintings they thought might sell. Two *did* sell, which gave me the confidence to submit paintings (via photos!) elsewhere. My work continued to sell, here and there, enough to pay for my beloved art supplies.

From my state of painting abandon, I developed a three-part theory. 1) Every painting or artistic creation, no matter what the personality thinks of it, is a love letter from true self. 2) Surrounding ourselves with our creations imprints the loving messages into our subconscious mind.

3) After enough imprints, the loving messages emerge into our personality's conscious awareness, where they become integrated into our perception of ourselves, others, and Life. With that theory in mind, I hung all my paintings where I would see them and get imprinted every day.

One night, nine months after the workshop, I sat on my living room floor basking in the paintings—or loving messages—that covered the walls. True self well-being began to fill me. My breath deepened and slowed; it became a joy to breathe. I felt relaxed and energized at the same time. Balance...it was balance! If cells could be happy, mine were. I could feel a chemical change occurring in my body, making me quietly happy, relaxed, alive, and balanced—and more so minute by minute. It never became too much (no jumping was necessary); it simply became more balanced. Soon I was feeling so good and so balanced that it dawned on me, "This is natural chemotherapy. We all need this. We're supposed to have this natural chemotherapy every day."

The next moment, my true self spoke. I heard clearly in my mind, the way I do when I'm doing true self channeling, "Start a free painting group for women with cancer."

I did. Three months later, in early 2000, the first group began its weekly meetings in my studio. It was attended by wonderful women turning to the healing power of creativity to face the challenge of a lifetime. Although I didn't talk about true self or do channeling or sounding, I used my true self perspective and techniques to help the women open to their true self creativity and effortlessly find their natural styles of painting.

Their paintings came flying out of them, released at last from the confines of "I'm not an artist." Fears, struggles, pain, and loneliness—as well as loves, dreams, joys, and camaraderie—shone from their paintings. It was all beauty to me. We adopted what I called the *Fabulous!* style of painting. Every painting, no matter how the painter's mind might be tempted to judge it, was *fabulous* to the group and celebrated as a perfect expression of something that had wanted to come out and be seen.

Some of the women with advanced cancer began to report, "The only time in my week I'm not in pain is when I'm here painting." I knew then that the group's creativity was tapping the unconditional, unwavering, true self well-being that is present in all of us at a level deeper than pain and suffering.

Months, then years, went by as we thrived in the flow of vibrant life and creative expression that filled the studio. I felt lucky to be there. The group grew, and new groups were added. Before I knew it, I was coordinating exhibits of cancer survivors' art, including the creation of two public sculptures. I organized the painting groups and art exhibits into Arts for Healing, a nonprofit project sponsored by a local hospital.

At the time of this writing in 2010, I still lead painting groups for Arts for Healing (www.ArtsforHealing.com)—and I joyfully continue my true self work teaching classes and doing private coaching. True self is a fountain of inspiration that carries me in multiple directions.

39

What Happened

From my first urge to paint, true self had been at the helm taking me in a direction my personality never could have predicted or designed. If someone had said to me in early 1999, "A few months from now you'll be painting," I wouldn't have believed them. If they had gone on to say, "A year from now you'll be selling your paintings, teaching painting in cancer support groups, and founding a nonprofit project to share the healing power of art," I would have thought them downright batty. At that time I did not think I had the ability to paint, and none of those activities would have even interested me. Yet as each of them unfolded, it became a treasure I loved with all my heart, enriching my life more than I ever could have imagined.

How did all that happen?

I had been nurturing my personality's connection with true self since 1984, which fast-tracked the development of gifts and skills I hadn't known were in me and brought them to the surface. Also, throughout those years, my ongoing true self channeling for clients fine-tuned my ability to follow true self guidance in my own life—the subtle nudges and as well as the stronger messages—which helped me to recognize my next steps as they appeared. As always, true self saw the bigger picture and offered it to me. I moved into it as I was ready.

To my surprise, the bigger picture included painting. While I painted in my studio, I used my techniques for opening to true self, which took me straight to my creative core, softened my inner critic, flowed love through me while I was painting, and freed me.

Like a luscious first lover, painting opened me to creative passion and carried me into territory once forbidden. As we do with first loves, I assumed I would remain in that relationship, with its full intensity, forever. Yet, as the relationship matured over the years, it changed. Fervor for my painting quieted and tapered off, and I fell increasingly in love with facilitating other people's creative unfolding in the painting groups. As I painted less, my creativity did not lessen, however. It remained strong and engaged. I discovered that my creativity was not in *painting*, it was in *me*.

I learned that creativity is not just a force to be expressed, but a source from which to live. My creativity engages every time I help people in a painting group, do true self channeling for a client or class, sound for myself, give a talk, negotiate a tense moment in a conversation or relationship, cook dinner, or simply navigate the rhythm of my day.

Creativity emanates from true self, infusing the body and personality in every moment. When we notice it, we usually think of it as *our* creativity, a quality we have and use. Yet *our* creativity is the same unlimited, intelligent force that is the creator of all things and all beings. Creativity is the material we are *made of*. We do not *have* creativity, we *are* Creativity itself.

LETTY PANG

Letty applied paint by the fistfuls. She had long ago stopped trying to make her paintings look like recognizable objects, people, or landscapes. She painted the interiors of herself, knowing that she didn't conform to any predictable images.

With hands protected by thin, latex gloves, Letty scooped big globs of acrylic paint from her palette or asked me to squirt tubes of purples, reds, and yellows directly onto her palms. For an hour or more she pressed paint onto her three- or four-foot-tall canvas, silent except for the occasional call, "More paint, please!" Chatter among other women in the cancer support, painting group seemed to glide in an arc around her, never entering or disturbing the globe of creative focus that was temporarily her world.

In that world, Letty was in a state of abandon. A dental hygienist by day, confined to the tiny, careful, and regimented tasks she accomplished in people's mouths, Letty became a painting superhero once a week in our group. No stroke was too bold, no canvas too tall, no emotion too deep for Letty. Her super power was *Expressing Herself Without Holding Back*.

Each week Letty would arrive exhausted from work, "I'm so tired I almost didn't come," and then fall into a state of creative reverie that was boundless. As she carried her completed painting out the door at the end of the evening, she'd say, "I knew I'd feel better if I came. I always do."

Whenever I asked Letty what her painting state felt like, she used words I've heard other people choose to describe their most profound, spiritual experiences: "Freedom, total freedom." "No effort." "Happy." "Fun." "I'm not thinking, I'm just experiencing." "Exploring." "It's not a doing, it's a happening." "A bigger part of me comes out." "There's big space inside me." "I feel all potentials happening at once." "Beauty." "Everything is okay."

Breast cancer and a mastectomy had brought Letty to the painting group. She had come thinking, "I can't paint," only to find out she simply hadn't finished the sentence: "I can't paint *anyone's way but my own*." When she did it her way, not only could Letty paint, she was set free.

Part VIII

LIVING THE SPLIT

Redefining Destiny

40

Heeding the Call

True self is calling to us from every cell in our bodies. Becoming conscious of true self is the destiny pulling each of us along our life's path. Sometimes we feel the pull and follow it easily and naturally. That is bliss. Other times there is surprising effort and the pain of bruised shins as we bump into obstacles in our way. Then there are the occasions when our path seems so thoroughly blocked that we feel stuck; and we fear we'll never get past that point.

The obstacles in our paths are creations of our limited beliefs and expectations of reality. As they spring out and take form in our lives, they get in our way and seem to thwart us. If we continue believing that these obstacles are real, and unrelated to us, we struggle with them. We try to resist, deny, overcome, or find a way around them, and we may even seem to succeed temporarily. Yet, limited beliefs and expectations are persistent, and they pop up as obstacles over and over again. As long as we hold limitations in our identity and our expectations of life, we will encounter them in our paths.

But take heart. Remember that unlimited spirit is at the core of everything, including your limited beliefs and expectations. Although the obstacles may seem like they are there to thwart you, they are not. They are markers placed at points of potential power for you. They are like signs saying, "Pause here, and make a shift." You can claim your power by shifting your awareness and recognizing something greater than the limitation that seems to be getting in your way.

Something greater, in this case, is choice. You have choice. You can choose to continue in your previous habituated pattern based on the personality's limitation, or you can choose to surrender to the unlimitedness of true self to create your path anew. Your destiny is a process rather than an outcome—a matter of following the vibrancy of life force rather than being in the right place at the right time doing the right thing. This is a destiny that has no particular form and is not dependent on specific events or situations for its expression.

There is no fixed map with a set path you are
to follow to make your life worthwhile.

There are no concrete ways to measure such things as success or failure. Destiny is less about the "proper" unfolding of your life and more about the innate unfolding of your being. As your being unfolds and you open to unlimitedness, your life will be touched and reshaped. In fact, the impulse to follow destiny's call will surface in every aspect of your life sooner or later and may prompt you to want to make significant changes. Yet, do not confuse the changes that occur with destiny itself.

Your life changes may begin with a feeling of dissatisfaction. It may be dissatisfaction with your work, your relationships, or any area of your life that involves your self-expression or interaction with the world. There is a feeling that you want deeper fulfillment in the situation and want to express or give more of who you truly are. The need to transform the current situation, or create a new one altogether, challenges you to continue drawing on deeper inner resources as you make your way.

Because most people find themselves at this type of crossroads in respect to their work, let's use work as the example in this chapter. Perhaps career is not the area that concerns you, but you long for a deeper, more expansive relationship, a more compatible circle of friends, or a new creative outlet. The information in this section can be applied to a variety of areas in your life where you feel the pull toward expanded change that has not yet fully manifested.

If work is your area of focus, perhaps you are yearning for a job that allows you to express more fully who you are and to make a direct, perceivable contribution to the world. This yearning can become a passion. You may sense your greater potential flowing through your body so strongly that it feels uncomfortable because you do not yet have the appropriate action for releasing it into the world. You are so ready to find your true work that you are about to pop—but you may not even know yet what the form of that work is. Months can go by without your getting any clearer about it! Still, the yearning and readiness, your greater destiny, continue to pull on you.

At such times, the inner readiness to move into a new level of unlimited living appears to outpace what is happening in your outer life. This incongruity between the inner and outer realities is one of many possible variations of the split we discussed in "Journey into Form." Remember that the split is the gap in the personality's awareness between the experience of limitation and the greater reality of unlimited being. In this case you are witnessing it as the gap between your growing inner awareness of unlimitedness and the circumstances in your life that still feel limiting.

In this version of the split, your job seems too limited to be a fulfilling expression of your greater self. As time passes, you may feel more expanded in your personal life yet even more empty and frustrated at work. Efforts to discover your new work may be unfruitful. You feel like you are spinning your wheels. Because you do not yet really know where you are going, it is understandable that you do not feel you are progressing in measurable ways.

After still more effort and frustration, you may begin turning your energy against yourself with self-sabotaging thoughts: "Something is wrong with me or I would have found my new work by now." "I am not trying hard enough." "I am not clear enough." "I should be more spiritual." "I should be more practical." In short, you have interpreted the existence of the split to mean that you are personally flawed in some way.

Or you may choose the flip side of that interpretation. Instead of being antagonistic to yourself, you may decide that the restriction originates outside yourself. "My problem exists because the world is not ready for what I have to offer." "Society is filled with density and limitation." "People's minds are closed to what I have to offer." "The economy is working against me." "The job I want doesn't exist. The world is not structured to allow people like me to make our contribution."

Both interpretations are based on the assumption that there is a flaw somewhere, and usually the flaw is one you cannot fix. The effect is the same regardless of whether you perceive the flaw as being within you or outside you; you are stymied by it. This adds a sense of inadequacy or incapacitation to the frustration you already feel. Clearly, a new option for relating to the situation is needed.

Although your personality will be searching, perhaps in frantic exasperation, for new outer action to take, the most powerful thing you can do at this point may simply be to accept that you are in the split and become more consciously present within it. Below are three basic steps for beginning this acceptance.

ATTUNEMENT
Accepting the Split

1. First, take some quiet time and attune to the potential you sense growing within. Feel it as it arises from your depths and fills you, streaming through every cell in your body. Notice how ready this energy is to go out into the world and carry the expansiveness and vitality of your true spirit into new work. Feel it as a passion, and cherish it.

2. Then, remember your feeling that the outer reality has not yet changed to match your inner readiness. Take time to notice how that feels. Feel the difference between your expansive inner readiness and the restriction that is still present in your outer life. Do not try to minimize the tension or discomfort of being caught in the split. Stay with yourself in it. Let the full spectrum of the experience be real.

3. Open to the love that you are. Remember that the unlimited love you are made of streams through you even while you experience both the expansiveness and the discomfort of the split. Perhaps think, "Even while I am in the split, I am unlimited love. I open to the unlimited love that I am."

Making time for this awareness is important. You may have a habit, as most people do, of trying to race through the split as quickly as possible. Your automatic reaction may be to rev up your energy and, using all the effort you can muster, attempt a flying leap across the split to the other side, where you hope your new work will be waiting. This exertion is an attempt to avoid the discomfort of living with the split.

You cannot successfully cross the split that way. You will find yourself stopped in the middle time and time again. Ironically, this is to your benefit.

As you resist the split and its discomfort,
you resist some aspect of yourself that knows
it needs to be included in your move forward
into more expansive living.

You continue to stop because the aspect of yourself that waits in the split is worth stopping for. It might be an aspect of yourself you are not conscious of that needs to be held close to your heart and carried with you into the creation of your new life. Perhaps it will even blossom and help you in essential ways when you get there.

One way to extend friendship to this sometimes elusive aspect of yourself is to settle into the split for awhile and feel what it is like. When you quit trying to leap the split and instead allow yourself to be in it, you no longer resist what is happening in the present in an effort to move ahead. Instead, you surrender to the present and to finding out what it can contribute to your journey. This makes all the difference.

It also changes your immediate goal. You still want your true work, of course; that intention need not weaken. Yet the primary goal becomes simply *being with whatever is revealing itself right now.* In this surrender, you notice that aliveness of your intention to find fulfilling work, and you also allow the discomfort of holding inner potential that has not yet come into fruition in the external world. You feel the split, which is preparation for gathering power.

41
Empowering Yourself with *Yearning* and *Not Knowing*

Spending time consciously in the split gives you the opportunity to face the blank slate of Not Knowing, which some people call "the void" or "emptiness". Not Knowing is an important—and powerful—ally. You have undoubtedly already sensed its power, but you may have been frightened of it and fled. Without understanding how to let it serve you, it is easy to fear Not Knowing as something that will weaken you and keep you from gaining clarity about your path.

Fear of Not Knowing may be part of what motivated you to continue trying to leap over the split. You may have resisted and avoided Not Knowing, assuming that giving in to it would leave you even more disoriented and lost than ever. When you are already frustrated or scared because you do not know what your new work is to be or how to find it, moving into a state of knowing even less may seem like the wrong direction entirely.

Not Knowing is not a lack of ideas. It is a clear, pure, open state of awareness that transcends personality and connects you with unlimited possibility. Fortunately, Not Knowing does not go away just because you don't recognize its value; it continues to offer itself. Yet, if you remain unaware of what it offers, you will continue resisting it and trying to fill its apparent emptiness. What will you try to fill it with? Knowing, of course.

When you fear Not Knowing, your natural defense is to try to know.

You will attempt to fill the Not Knowing with thoughts and ideas that you hope will get you to your new work. Personality is uncomfortable with open-ended questions and soothes itself by coming up with answers. Similarly, it is uncomfortable with the apparent emptiness of the split and tries to fill it with tangibles. Personality believes that the way to find your new work is to stay in control, in this case to "know" your way there. It is not aware of how much more empowering and enriching it can be to "not know" your way there.

Not Knowing is a powerful state of being that transcends the thoughts and ideas generated by your intellect. The intellect is in the personality, and can create only according to the limitation it has already known. In your longing for true work, you are asking for work that is greater than the work you have already known. To find it, you must open to a state of awareness greater than the awareness you have already known. Ironically, one way to go beyond what you have known is to go into Not Knowing; there you are wide open.

Personality's knowing automatically screens out possibilities that are unfamiliar. Not Knowing does not limit you to the possibilities your intellect can create or your personality can plan; it opens you to the unlimited.

The yearning to find your true work (or relationship or creativity) is a variation on the desire for true self and is, therefore, another pure state we'll call *true yearning*. Allowing true yearning and Not Knowing *together* creates the beginning of something new and more expanded in your life. It is not so much the marriage of true yearning and knowing, but the marriage of true yearning and Not Knowing that yields the greatest possibility.

MEDITATION
Yearning and Not Knowing

1. Close your eyes, and allow yourself to breathe gently and easily.... Follow a few breaths into your throat area.... Follow a few breaths into your heart area.... Follow a few breaths into your belly.... Assume that your breath is gently and easily taking you into your true self....

2. As you continue to breathe gently and easily into true self, allow your yearning to surface.... You may feel your yearning passionately or you

may barely feel it at all; it makes no difference. It is not the sensation that is important. It is your intent. When your intent is to allow your yearning to surface, it will happen whether you feel it or not....

3. Continue to sense the yearning as it is.... Now also invite the Not Knowing to present itself. Notice the Not Knowing.

4. Not Knowing may appear as a blank screen, an empty hole, a beautiful light, or as something else. It may even come as nothing at all: no image or feeling or sense of anything. Open to it in whatever way it presents itself....

5. Allow the yearning and Not Knowing to spend time with you together.... Breathe gently and easily into the yearning and Not Knowing, allowing yourself to trust their presence....

6. When you are ready to come out of meditation, turn your awareness to your whole body, noticing how it feels from head to toe.... Then slowly stretch, and open your eyes.

42
Empowering Your Speech

Everything you say affects your consciousness, either affirming or changing your habits of thinking. When your statements allow room for new and fulfilling possibilities, you affirm your true self and can receive its guidance. But when you speak with restriction, you identify with your personality's focus on limitation and trigger your thoughts to continue along a narrow track.

For example, if your personality resists Not Knowing and is anxious for the security of concrete answers, you may automatically say, "I just don't know what to do. I wish I knew!" Immediately your mind will go to work looking for answers, trying to fill the Not Knowing with knowing. Then you miss the opportunity to expand.

To practice talking about your yearning and Not Knowing in ways that reinforce your openness to unlimited possibilities, take some time to sit and use the following conversational guidelines with a trusted friend. It is important that this person agrees to listen without giving you verbal feedback, advice, or suggestions. The ability to listen and receive your experience is her or his greatest contribution.

ATTUNEMENT
Talking about Yearning and Not Knowing

1. Begin by describing your yearning. Open your heart and tell how it feels. If you have visions, emotions, physical feelings, or sensations of energy that come from the yearning, describe them. Your yearning is valuable: treat it as a treasure you are showing your friend.

2. After you speak about your yearning, spend just as much time describing the Not Knowing. Allow the Not Knowing to present itself to you in its strength and openness. Describe it in detail to your friend, and do not try to fill its emptiness. Sitting with its emptiness may bring you to its spaciousness and beauty. For example, you may say something like, "The Not Knowing is just blank space, empty space." Next you may find yourself saying, "You know, this emptiness really gives me the time I need to avoid rushing into something. I can move more slowly and consciously."

Of course, what you actually say may be quite different, but the important things are these: (a) Let Not Knowing present itself to you on its own terms; (b) Recognize Not Knowing as your ally; (c) Communicate your full experience; (d) Let yourself speak with the assumption that Not Knowing has purpose. You do not have to know what its purpose is right now. You just need to be receptive to Not Knowing—to what is real and trustworthy about it.

43
Setting Your Course

Any path of transformation will bring you to unexpected crossroads. Practical decisions must be made. In which direction should you go? What actions should you take? Whom should you choose as traveling companions? As your goals and values change, your old criteria for making choices may seem feeble or irrelevant. If you do not yet see exactly where you are headed, you may feel doubly at a loss. When you are caught in uncertainty and confusion but have decisions to make, how can you make the wisest choices?

The Not Knowing can help. Although the intellect likes to think that information comes from knowing, most of your true information comes directly from Not Knowing. As we just discussed, if you rely solely on knowing, you are limited by the confines of what your personality perceives or has already experienced. For staying on one plane of awareness, the knowing is exceedingly helpful; for expanding into new territory, the Not Knowing is a greater resource.

To make a choice, first sit with the Not Knowing. Spend time with it. Make your peace with it. Allow yourself to notice your impatience or inclination to hurry through Not Knowing because of insecurity or fear. When you are out of touch with true self, you are particularly vulnerable to fear and to the need to grab at things to do to give yourself a sense of comfort or security. The feeling is, "*That* will make me safe. *That* will make me okay. Doing *that* will make me happy." Or, you may have the panicky thought, "If I don't find the right thing to do soon, I'm going to be in a lot of trouble!"

Noticing your version of this inner dialogue is helpful because it gives you unmistakable feedback that you are identifying with limitation. When you catch yourself in that pattern, take a breath and give compassion to the part of your personality that is suffering because it is out of touch with true self. Compassionate presence will help more than answers in that moment.

You came into physical form to be human and,
from the midst of human limitation,
to open to unlimited being.

To complete your life purpose you must accept being fully human, which includes living in limitation. A response of fear, panic, and looking to externals for the power that actually comes from true self is proof you are living the limited aspect of humanness well. Do not be afraid of this. The pure longing to complete your life purpose is so strongly inherent in your being that it will continue to pull you onward no matter how thoroughly submerged in the limited you have become.

After you recognize that the sense of urgency comes from your personality and you extend compassion to it, take another deep breath and gently turn to the longing and Not Knowing as your guidance about what to do. This lifts the decision from the hands of the small self that is trying to stay in control and gives it to the greater self, from which a decision of true empowerment can be made.

How can you do this? One way is to become comfortable with the "Yearning and Not Knowing" meditation described at the end of the "Gathering Power" chapter, and then to add some steps for offering your choices to Not Knowing. The lengthened meditation is listed below.

MEDITATION
Yearning, Not Knowing, and Decisions

1. Close your eyes, and allow yourself to breathe gently and easily. . . . Follow a few breaths into your throat area. . . . Follow a few breaths into your heart area. . . . Follow a few breaths into your belly. . . . Assume that your breath is gently and easily taking you into your true self. . . .

2. As you continue to breathe gently and easily into true self, allow your yearning to surface. . . . You may feel your yearning passionately or

you may barely feel it at all; it makes no difference. It is not the sensation that is important. It is your intent. When your intent is to allow your yearning to surface, it will happen whether you feel it or not. . . .

3. Continue to sense the yearning as it is.. . . . Now also invite the Not Knowing to present itself. Notice the Not Knowing. . . .

4. Not Knowing may appear as a blank screen, an empty hole, a beautiful light, or as something else. It may even come as nothing at all: no image or feeling or sense of anything. Open to it in whatever way it presents itself. . . .

5. Allow the yearning and Not Knowing to spend time with you together. . . . Breathe gently and easily into the yearning and Not Knowing, allowing yourself to trust their presence. . . .

6. Hand one of your choices to Not Knowing, and say, "What about this possibility?" You are giving that possibility to Not Knowing so it can reflect a greater perspective to you. . . .

7. Allow Not Knowing to reveal the essence of that choice to you. That choice may start vibrating with life or it may become duller, faded, or deadened—or something else may happen. Spend a few moments observing the feeling or image that is presented. . . .

When you have received the message about that possible choice, put that choice aside and hand Not Knowing the next one. You can repeat the process until you have gotten energetic feedback on all the choices you are considering. If you have several choices to present to Not Knowing and become fatigued before you get through them all, simply take a break until you are rested. Then repeat the meditation for the remaining choices.

8. When you are ready to come out of meditation, turn your awareness to your whole body, noticing how it feels from head to toe. . . . Then slowly stretch, and open your eyes.

The feedback from Not Knowing may be specific images that you immediately understand, or it may be more abstract or subtle. You may have to go entirely by how you feel. With practice you will become more adept at understanding the "language" you share with Not Knowing. You can then consider the information you receive from Not Knowing as you weigh your choices and make your decisions.

If each possibility looks or feels wonderful as Not Knowing reflects the energy back to you, consider that perhaps you cannot make a mistake in your choice. In fact, even though you may not be consciously aware of it, any decision you make comes from some important part of yourself that wants expression. As you follow through on a decision, whether it turns out to bring you joy or sorrow, abundance or loss, or a combination of experiences, some aspect of your being wanted to be expressed, or manifested, and you gave it expression by making that choice. Manifesting and interacting with that aspect of self via the situation you created from that choice exposes you to learning that can enable you to grow and move on.

Sometimes it is better to make a decision and see what happens than to be forever afraid of making the wrong choice. The most important thing is simply that you come fully to life while you are here in this world. Any choice you make carries that possibility.

44
Updating the Map

As you lovingly accept your personality, become familiar with your emotions, and take counsel from Not Knowing, a new vision may develop that allows you to look more honestly and creatively at your life. You may begin to question the unnecessary judgments and restrictions you have placed on yourself and others over the years. You may want to release outdated emotional or behavioral patterns you adopted for survival at earlier stages of your life that are not empowering now. How can you do this?

Transformation occurs more smoothly and deeply when you extend compassion and love to yourself. Think about loving yourself for a moment. For some people, the mere idea of loving themselves is overwhelming; it seems like too big a job. They unconsciously assume they are so unlovable by nature that any efforts to love themselves would be exhausting or would simply fail. They think they have to conjure feelings of love, love, love that never stop. What an arduous task!

If you feel that loving yourself is difficult, you can do four things:

ATTUNEMENT
Finding Affection for Self

1. Remember the love that you are. When you remember that unlimited love is always vibrant and alive in every cell of your body, it is easier to feel some love for yourself. Love is something that already radiates through you, not something you have to create on the spot.

2. Think in terms of simply having some affection for yourself. Affection seems easier, as though it is a scaled-down expression of love. It is tiny love. In your most self-critical moments, you do not have to stretch so far to find a tiny feeling of affection for yourself, yet the benefit of that affection will be just as great as if you were enthusiastically in love with yourself. Let tiny love—or a very subtle feeling of affection—be enough.

3. As you catch yourself repeating your old pattern, take a moment to ask, "Where is my affection for myself in this situation?" As you continue asking, gently and with genuine sincerity, you will find affection. Even if the old pattern is one of self-hatred or self-criticism, which is terribly uncomfortable, it is still possible to find some inner affection for who you are. It may help to imagine that you are stepping back far enough for a greater perspective. Or, imagine that you are seeing with bigger eyes, eyes that can find even the tiniest affection for self, no matter how hidden it may be.

4. Do *Sweet Me*. Whether you are sitting quietly or doing something, silently say the words *Sweet Me* and let them drop into you, as though you are dropping pebbles into a pond. Assume *Sweet Me* will automatically settle within you, wherever it is needed. You do not need to feel sweet or loving. You are simply letting *Sweet Me* settle alongside whatever you are feeling. With that understanding, drop Sweet Me's into yourself a few more times, with at least a breath or two between them.

Let's take a moment to examine what it is like to be caught in an outdated pattern or emotion or behavior. You want to change it, but you feel like it will never fade. Looking closely, we find the same two elements we discussed earlier: true yearning and Not Knowing. You yearn for a more expanded way of being that expresses your true self, yet you do not know whether the restrictive pattern will ever change or how that change may happen. In short, you are in a split!

Joining you there is the small self (personality) who wants to stay in control. Personality wants to leap over the split as soon as possible and will try to do it by taking immediate action to avoid, deny, reject, or dismantle the restrictive pattern. These efforts, based on control, are rarely effective and most often lead to frustration and an increase in the discomfort of being caught in the split.

What can you do? Once again, you will be most effective by being present with yourself and honest about how you feel. "Here I am in the split again, and this is uncomfortable." When you no longer try to flee, you can witness the pattern you have been caught in "(I'm *still* doing this"), feel the yearning, ("I want a new way of being that comes from my true self rather than from old, restrictive conditioning"), and let the Not Knowing be with you ("I don't know how to make this pattern change, but I'm open and committed to it happening").

Being in the split is like sitting on top of a pyramid;
whether or not you can feel it,
all energies are aligned to give you power.

Because the predominant feelings in the split are often helplessness, fear, and frustration, the power available to you is easily overlooked and misdirected. Yet whether you are conscious or unconscious about what you are doing, whatever you do will carry power. If you resist the split, your resistance will be amplified, reinforcing the sense of being caught in a struggle. This will not help you to change the pattern that originally distressed you. If, however, you compassionately allow yourself to feel the longing for change and the feelings that go with being in the split (discomfort, anticipation, excitement, fear, etc.), the creative energies of both your longing and your willingness to be present with yourself will be empowered for you. As you also open to Not Knowing, your ability to draw from the unlimited Source will be strengthened, and new possibilities can come to you.

With this kind of receptivity and empowerment, you are open to transformation and are attuning to your greater potential. In time you may need to take specific actions to support your personality in its change. Proceed, knowing that whatever you genuinely want for yourself and are willing to create through the assistance of true self is possible.

Your destiny is not preordained by some outside source. It is inside you, created and re-created in every moment by your own unbounded self. It is as fluid and transmutable as you are. If you do not like where you are going or the weight of the baggage you carry, you can make revisions. You do this not by resisting or controlling what you find on your path, but by directing your awareness. Unlimited possibilities await you.

45

Getting Free of Self-Judgment

Feeling separate from the love that you are makes you easy prey to self-judgment. Self-judgment is unrelenting; it never strikes just once, but uses your thoughts to attack again and again. Sooner or later these self-rejecting thoughts can invalidate everything about who you are and the path you are on, leaving you disoriented and confused. Heavy with doubt, you drag your feet and wonder why life isn't more rewarding. This is a sign that it is time to expand your perception.

As painful and restricting as self-rejecting thoughts can be, they are not all bad. There is an energy at the core of each that you can use to your advantage, no matter how crippling the content of the thought may be. You can view that core energy as hidden nourishment that is yours to claim. When you are caught in self-sabotaging thoughts, the following three steps can help you become present and aware enough to use that energy constructively.

ATTUNEMENT
Facing Self-Judgment

1. Stop for a moment and realize that self-rejecting thoughts are occurring. It will not help you to ignore them or passively accept them. It *will* help you to acknowledge their presence.

2. Let yourself feel how uncomfortable it is to have your energy turned against yourself. Notice that not only is it a mental discomfort, but also it feels uncomfortable to your body to be bathed with critical thought.

3. Use the power of your intention: Gently and clearly state that you want the energy within the self-rejecting thoughts to bring you a greater experience of true self.

——————————————— ♡ ———————————————

So there you are, noticing a painfully critical thought, and feeling the emotional and physical discomfort it causes. From the midst of it, you remind yourself of what you want: "Even in this criticism and discomfort, I want this thought to bring me to a greater experience of true self." Or, to be more accurate, say, "I want the *energy* of this thought to bring me to a greater experience of true self." The distinction between the thought and its energy is important. It is not the content of the thought that will bring you to true self, but the energy at the core of it.

You want to align yourself with the power—the core energy—of thought.

Energy exists at the core of all thoughts, feelings, things, and living creatures. All creation—whether you experience it as pleasant or unpleasant, good or bad, limited or unlimited—carries in its essence the unlimited love and creativity of vibrant life force. The content of any thought is always secondary to the unlimited love, creativity, and life force the thought carries at its core. That is why "negative" thoughts work as well as "positive" ones for opening you to true self—*if you remember to transcend the content and go to the core energy.*

All thoughts spring from Source. Source is unlimited, unconditional love and well-being. Source is all possibility. The more you are immersed in the experience of Source, the more you are immersed in unlimited love, all possibility, and absolute well-being, regardless of what is happening in your life and regardless of what you are thinking. What a beautiful irony to find Source even through your self-critical thoughts! This is easy to do and is excellent practice for opening to true self. What seems most real and true to the judgmental mind actually carries the least power and truth if you shift your awareness to a deeper level.

Judgmental thought can be destructive if you stay at the content level. Believing the content damages your self-image and hurts your personality. On the other hand, resisting or rebelling against judgmental thought is depleting because you are always fighting a losing battle. Even if you try to defend against the content of self-judgment by countering with turnaround statements such as, "No, I'm not bad, I'm good" or "There's nothing wrong with me. I'm really okay," the judgmental thinking starts up again the moment you stop your defense. Then you must leap into battle again and again. It is an exhausting war.

The war dissolves and the harm turns to healing when you no longer engage with the content of self-rejecting thoughts but go straight to the Source energy within them that will nurture you. You free yourself from being victimized by self-judgment, and self-judgment becomes, like everything else, just another vehicle to reconnect you with Source.

Source is always the healing.

When it becomes your habit to choose Source in the midst of self-rejection, that shift changes your entire relationship with the world. By disengaging from the content of self-rejecting thought and choosing to be empowered and carried forward by the Source energy at its core, you transcend limitation and align with unlimitedness. You open to true self. As you develop this new pattern, you will find yourself automatically applying this transcendence to other situations in your life as well.

To see how this happens, take a moment to imagine a threatening situation, one in which you feel boxed into a corner and cannot get out. You are trapped, feeling that something terrible is happening to you, yet you are helpless to stop it. Notice that feeling. It is similar to the feeling created in your body when your thoughts are harshly judgmental of yourself; your body feels the pain of the self-hostility and the distress of not being able to get away from it.

Now imagine that even though you are trapped, you are able to remember the love that you and to reconnect in another way with your true self. As you do this, your fear and pain soften, and your body slowly relaxes into ease and joy. It is safe to be expansive. You know that your well-being is assured regardless of what is happening externally. You sense that the core energy of everything in the situation around you—

including the corner you were boxed into—is a carrier of the unlimited love and life force of Source.

By going through this kind of shift—transcending to Source, or true self, whenever the distress of self-judgment occurs—your body and personality learn transcendence as a new pattern. After enough repetition, the shift will happen automatically and increase in its scope. As you become used to transcending to Source in the midst of the distress of self-judgment, transcendence to Source will also be triggered in other situations that create the same type of distress in your body.

It is wonderful when this shift becomes automatic. It means you are naturally seeking the unlimited in the midst of limitation. Sometimes this will occur in such subtle ways that you do not consciously notice it. Other times it will be a delightful surprise. As it becomes second nature, you will rejoice at the well-being it brings you.

CHERIE DETER McARTHUR

Cherie was a mild mannered bookkeeper with a big dream: She wanted to live in paradise. Tired of city life in California and work that didn't make her heart sing, or even hum, her daydreams carried her to Hawaii. She longed to see the lush green of jungle, inhale warm, moist, tropical air, and live in a slower rhythm that brought her close to the land.

Her dream started to come true in 1990 when she and her husband, Ian, packed up their two kids and moved to the Big Island of Hawaii. Cherie became a flower vendor, selling to tourists who poured off the cruise ships in port, and worked part-time in a nursery.

In 1996 Cherie and Ian bought a 10-acre macadamia nut farm. Or the remnants of one. Long neglected and reclaimed by the jungle, the 12-foot trees were barely visible. They had to be *uncovered* before they could be worked. Thick grasses as tall as the trees filled the orchards. Jungle vines two inches in diameter gripped the tree trunks and branches, twisting their way to the tree tops for light.

Ian's career creating special effects for Hollywood movies financed the purchase of the farm but took him out of state for months at a time. So Cherie rolled up her sleeves and got to work. She learned how to use a machete and scythe and attacked the grasses towering over her head. She took on the jungle single-handedly—literally. Cherie had been born with a right arm that stopped just below the elbow, so she had only one hand. That had never stopped her before, so why would it now?

Even with the help of men Cherie hired, it took two years of hard labor, slashing and removing the grasses, then hacking the vines and unwinding them from the 600 trees, to ready the farm. In 1998 Cherie's dream was realized as Puna Girl Farms went into production of macadamia nuts and macadamia flower honey.

Puna Girl Farms was good for Cherie's soul. The hard work continued, but she loved it. For nine years she and her workers mowed the tenacious orchard grass, pruned and fertilized the trees, gathered the nuts, and delivered the harvest to a processor. After each tropical storm screamed across the island, they cleared away broken branches and fallen trees. They battled wild pigs who damaged the orchard, and when it seemed the pigs might win, erected an electric fence to keep them off the farm. Cherie ended every day dog tired, but her heart sang anyway.

In early 2007 the bottom fell out. The price of macadamia nuts plummeted to a low that hadn't been seen in generations. Suddenly Cherie stood to lose her farm. The cost of picking the nuts would so extremely exceed the price she could get at market that she was unable to harvest her crop. She couldn't afford to take her crop to market for such a loss, couldn't afford to pull out the trees and plant something else, and couldn't afford to do nothing. Cherie was stuck.

People recommended selling her land. Cherie loved her farm. It was her dream come true, and she had worked hard for it. She didn't want to lose it. And her employees depended on her; she didn't want to put them out of work. Cherie couldn't figure out a solution. Or, more accurately, her *personality* couldn't figure out a solution. So Cherie took the issue to someone who could: her true self.

Cherie turned to techniques she had learned in my *Living from True Self* class, which had met throughout the previous year. She sat quietly, did a few minutes of sounding, and then imagined that her breath was breathing her, gently and easily, into true self. To true self she said, "This farm needs to pay for itself. What can I do? I turn it over to you. Show me what I can do." As she continued breathing into true self, an answer came: "You are in a state of confusion, but there are simple answers. Visualize what you want, and proceed. Your wanting has strength."

A few days later, Cherie again sat quietly, sounded, and imagined that her breath was breathing her into true self. Again an answer came: "Don't worry, let go, receive. Things are already being taken care of by your true self."

Cherie, used to relying on a plan and her own hard work to execute it, was in new territory. It was the territory of yearning (or wanting) and Not Knowing. She wanted to save the farm yet didn't know how to do it. Wanting was familiar to her. Proceeding in a state of Not Knowing about something this important was new and disorienting. Cherie had turned to true self to learn how to navigate Not Knowing.

True self had let her know that goodness was in the works, goodness that was greater than anything her personality could see from its limited perspective or make happen on its own. With the message "Don't worry, let go, receive," true self hadn't been suggesting that Cherie become passive, but had been guiding her to develop a state of open receptivity. As long as her action-oriented personality was dominating, she couldn't see her deeper path or receive the greater goodness waiting there for her. A well-developed state of receptivity and new roots into true self would help her to find her way and gain the most from it.

During the next few weeks, stress, worry, and panic about the farm's situation visited Cherie several times a day. Each time, remembering true self's messages, she chose not to be controlled by her personality's distress, but instead to turn toward her true self well-being, even if she could not yet see how that well-being would manifest in her life. When the distress tapped her on the shoulder, she didn't deny or reject it; she just reminded herself, "I've already asked for true self's help. I believe in it. I'm open to it." Or she would take a breath into true self. Or she would turn her thoughts to something enjoyable that helped her remain open to well-being.

Each time she gently chose well-being over her personality's reaction of distress, relief flowed through her body immediately. She felt happier and lighter. Stomach problems and stress headaches that had begun to plague her disappeared.

As Cherie practiced her new well-being process, it became easier and more automatic. She also found worry and distress occurring with decreasing frequency and her well-being lasting longer. For example, early on she felt happy and balanced for maybe an hour between episodes of worry. A few days later she felt happy and balanced for two hours between episodes of worry. Within a few more days it was up to three hours, and so on until happiness and balance were lasting all day. Worry and distress were taking a back seat to well-being.

One evening six weeks after Cherie had started her well-being process, she and Ian were sipping cocktails in the area of the farm they called "the park." The park was two acres of cleared land that had no trees, just lush, mowed grass on top of a hill that offered gorgeous views overlooking other farms and the ocean. It was their haven.

"This is such a beautiful spot," Cherie mused, "and this view is *amazing*. People would love it. There's just *got* to be something we can do with all this beauty to save the farm."

They had had this conversation before. Ian grinned and repeated the new catch phrase they had coined in a similarly wistful moment a few nights earlier, "Build a pavilion, and they will come."

Later in the week Cherie was talking with the receptionist in her chiropractor's office about her dilemma. "We're trying to figure out something to do with the park. Do you have any ideas?"

The receptionist took in a quick breath and held it for a moment. "You're giving me goose bumps," she said. "Part of the week I work for a tour company that's looking for a place to take tourists for their picnic lunches. I think your park would be perfect! Most of our tourists have never seen a macadamia farm."

Days later the owners of the tour company met Cherie in "the park," set up picnic tables under canopies, and handed Cherie a schedule. Soon they started bringing their tours to Puna Girl Farms for lunch. Cherie became the first "real, live macadamia farmer" most of the tourists had ever met, and she happily stepped into the role. Chatting about the farm she loved so much, selling her honey, and giving samples of her macadamia nuts plus the bananas, star fruit, pineapples, and lychee that also grew on her property made her happy. Cherie realized that not only had she achieved her dream of living in paradise, now she was sharing it with people from all over the world. Yes, her true self definitely had known what to do.

In the following months the size and frequency of the tours increased, and Cherie and Ian built their pavilion. Enough income was generated for the farm workers to remain employed; they maintained the orchards and kept the jungle at bay so nut production would be ready to resume whenever prices should go back up. The farm was saved!

But there was more to it than that. Cherie had used the crisis for the purpose it had manifested: to deepen her personality's roots in true self and to take her dream, the farm in paradise, to its next level. Her personality could not have seen the big picture or have figured out the details for making it happen. It had been a plan so big it could only have been orchestrated by true self.

Cherie had succeeded by learning that Not Knowing was not a weak or passive state but a state of profound receptivity in which goodness was percolating for her; by turning over her dilemma to true self and opening to true self's guidance; and by choosing deeper well-being in the face of stress and worry. Cherie had found a new way to navigate into abundance,

Visit Cherie, Ian, and Puna Girl Farms at www.PunaGirlFarms.com

Part IX

AWAKENED PERSONALITY

Loyal Servant to Unlimited Spirit

46
Transformation and Perfection

Living your life as an ongoing process of transformation is a marvelous adventure. In facing the challenges that come your way, you gain inner strength, develop emotional depth and agility, and learn to transcend limitation that may otherwise continue to lock you into patterns of struggle and unhappiness.

Yet, as with everything, there is a need for balance. An over-reliance on transformation can be an addiction, which occurs when people continuously focus on change because they cannot accept themselves as they are. Because the motivation for this kind of transformation is self-rejection, these efforts toward change become a distraction from being with self. Here are some pitfalls of this pattern:

1. No matter how much change is made, it is never enough to be fully satisfying.

2. Because the change that has been made was not based on the unconditional self-love and well-being of true self, it turns out to be disappointingly limited in its scope or does not last.

3. The basic issue of self-rejection is avoided and is never resolved.

Transformation addition may be directed inward (changing the self) or outward (changing the world) and often carries a tone of life or death urgency. The basic assumption of the inner directed pattern is, "I must change to be okay." The outer directed pattern is, "The world (or other people) must change for me to be okay."

Inner directed dialogue may include statements like the following: "To grow or heal, I must change." "To get along better with people or to manifest money or to contribute to the world—I must change." "To live with myself, I must become something better than what I already am." Outer directed dialogue may be about the same issues, but with the assumption that it is other people or the world that must change rather than (or at least more than) the self.

The need to change yourself (or anyone else) to attain well-being leaves you at a definite disadvantage. It means living with emptiness and insecurity while you try to become (or get someone else to become) whatever you think is better. The effort you expend to create this change can be endless and exhausting.

This does not mean you should give up on transformation and be stuck with inner patterns and outer circumstances that do not feel right to you. Growth and change are important. It may be helpful, however, to take an honest look at the attitude that motivates your change. If the beliefs about yourself that prompt your change are healthy, the changes you make will support your greater health. If those beliefs are self-rejecting, your changes, no matter how dramatic, will have limited benefit.

What if the real truth is that you are enough right now, just as you are? What if well-being is your birthright and will come alive for you in an instant if you are willing to let yourself have it? What if all change and transformation in you and in the world are options but not necessities?

Understand that from unlimited spirit's perspective, there is nothing wrong with you; you are perfect as you are. You do not have a flaw or a blemish. Even your suffering or the suffering of others is not a sign that anything needs to be fixed. Everything carries perfection as it is.

Although your personality may find this
difficult to accept or believe,
nothing about you or the world needs
to be changed for well-being to occur.

Vibrant life force, unconditional love, and unlimited well-being flow through all things, all beings, and all situations as they are right now. These qualities already exist everywhere. Everyone and everything are made of them, although this truth is often overlooked.

If tomorrow, every person on earth were to open consciously to the vibrant life force, unconditional love, and unlimited well-being of Source, there would be an instant shift in consensus about what should be done in the world. There no longer would be panic, urgency, or resistance about making change. Instead there would be the knowing that Source is present and available everywhere, in the biggest disasters as much as in the most beautiful creations of nature. People would make change from pure choice and well-being rather than from urgency and suffering. Their energies would go into creating an environment for all creatures that expresses the great well-being that already exists.

This intent is different than trying to change things so people can escape suffering. The experience of suffering is real, but that does not mean it carries the greatest truth. Its reality is based in the personality's orientation to limitation and separation. Actions taken to escape suffering reinforce the belief in suffering as a foundational force of existence.

Recognize that when you identify with life at a superficial level, you are focused within the illusion of limitation, which is where suffering is perceived and experienced. At that level, your actions may bring change to the forms in which suffering occurs, but suffering will not be eliminated as long as you believe in it and relate to it at that level.

Well-being is the natural state
of true self and unlimited spirit.

If you want to transform suffering, bring your awareness to the well-being that already *is* at the deepest level. There, free from suffering, you can make choices and changes from a pure sense of inner peace, regardless of the external situation. Your actions will then carry unlimited creative power and will continue to reveal well-being as the most basic reality.

If you feel urgency about creating change in your life or in the world, you probably do not experience yourself as a vehicle for Source: vibrant life force, unconditional love, and unlimited well-being. You may be focusing on change to compensate for this lack. Creating change becomes a replacement for what you want most deeply but do not have. Yet, because it is more superficial, making change in yourself or others is much less satisfying than having the full experience of source. When you are in separation from Source, the change you make—in yourself, in someone else, in the world—is never quite enough. There is always more that calls to you with that familiar urgency.

Again, by no means is this a suggestion that you should stop trying to create change or take action to relieve suffering. Being passive and ineffective in the world is no solution to missing your connection with Source. However, you may need to face your longing for the inner peace of deep connection.

> *There is one way to tell easily and instantly*
> *whether you feel separate from Source:*
> *The degree to which you feel distress in your life*
> *is the degree to which you are in separation.*

It is important to distinguish between *feeling* separate from Source and *being* separate from Source. There is no such thing as actually being separate, because Source, or true self, is in every aspect of yourself and your world. For our purposes, being in separation simply means losing conscious awareness of the presence of Source, orienting instead to your personality's reality of separation, limitation, and, therefore, suffering.

47

Nurturing Your Personality

Because the personality is such a strong part of your experience of self, you need to take good care of it. This includes honoring it by recognizing its needs and giving it a healthy environment, internally and externally. When you consider making changes in your life, the following four steps may be helpful.

ATTUNEMENT
Creating Changes in Your Life

1. Begin by dropping the idea of changing yourself to become a better person.

2. Assume for the moment that you are okay as you are and that you can have well-being right now without making any internal or external changes.

3. From that clear space ask yourself, "What does my personality need to be its healthiest?"

4. Make a list of the top one to five actions you can take—or inner changes you can make—that will support your personality in living in well-being and goodness.

You may discover that your personality needs more companionship with supportive friends, more love, a change in your work environment, more play and enjoyment, a sense of accomplishment or challenge, a healthier body, more self-expression, new creative outlets, or greater attention to your emotions, to name a few possibilities. For example, your personality may ask you to deepen specific friendships you already have and let go of others, or perhaps to persevere in finding new friends who suit you better.

Or, because your body is home to your personality, you may need to give more attention and care to your body. Just as you would not want to live in a house that falls apart, you do not want to put your personality into a body that falls apart from lack of care. You may need to choose foods and activities that will nurture and strengthen your body so your personality can live in a clean, strong, supportive physical environment.

Proper emotional care of self is as important as proper eating and exercise. Your personality may tell you that you need a deeper understanding of your emotional responses. It may also ask for new options to replace old patterns that no longer serve you; a release of feelings you have been holding back for too long; greater compassion for yourself; or a good pat on the back to validate the emotional growth you have already begun.

You may be able to get your emotional needs met through contact with friends whom you trust to live in truth with you, through a good therapist or support group, or through meaningful involvement with your community. Be sure to find your source for healthy emotional interaction and growth if your personality requests it. You need open, clear, strong emotional circuitry that serves you in the world.

Tending to your personality's needs
is the basic housekeeping required
for a healthy human being.

How much housekeeping is needed? Emotional clearing, proper diet and exercise, and healthy rapport with family, friends, and community all nurture the personality. Yet even these health-enhancing actions are completely fulfilling only when accompanied by attunement to spirit.

Spirit is the Source from which personality manifests. For balanced living, the vehicle of expression (personality) must be strongly developed, but it must not be mistaken for the greater consciousness that is doing the expressing (spirit). It is unlimited spirit that links us in unity to all things and all beings; personality on its own cannot do this.

Consider the imbalances that occur when either personality or spirit is ignored. Some people who are strongly oriented to personality ignore spirit and draw on its power only as a last resort. Their over reliance on personality keeps them focused in limitation, creating a life of illusion, materialism, judgment, and attachment. On the other hand, some spiritually oriented people recognize only the value of spirit and deny or resist the importance of personality. This disconnection from personality makes it difficult for their expansive awareness to integrate into daily life at the practical levels, so they often have trouble getting their material needs met or feel they don't belong in the world.

Personality's highest function is as a vehicle for spirit.

A weakened personality is less able to tolerate the brilliant vibration of spirit, while a healthy personality carries it easily. Because your personality is focused in the physical world, its consciousness affects your everyday view of the world. Supporting the health of your personality increases your capacity for bringing the brilliance of spirit through your personality into your life.

As your healthy personality opens to true self, you surrender to the unlimited. In that alignment there is total well-being; nothing exists that is not well-being. Even a situation in your life that may normally cause you intense suffering is removed of all distress when viewed from this state of true self well-being. Such a situation becomes infused instead with unlimited love, compassion, and surrender to the sublime beauty of life. Suffering is replaced by the knowing that nothing is essentially wrong and that only perfection exists. Your attachment to anything outside yourself you had hoped would save you from suffering is automatically dropped. You are already saved, for you are one with Source.

48
Where Is Your Support?

Have you found your unshakable source of support yet? Without it, life can be overwhelming and your path can seem impossibly long or rocky. No matter how rough the going, you need to know that you are cared for and guided and that there is a power supporting you that will not let you down.

Ask yourself, "Where is my truest, most reliable support right now?" You may think of support from specific people in your life, but go deeper. Where is support that is even more constant and profound than what another person can give you? Where is support that goes beyond the security you can get from money or a satisfying career? Where is support that is continuous, never wavering for a moment? You are looking for support that is undiminished by anything that happens around you, by what other people say or do, or by what you gain or lose in the world. You are looking for Source.

Where can you find Source? It is the unlimited; it is everywhere. True self is your link to it, so look within. As you allow true self to become more real to you, you find divine support around you and within you that is absolutely unthreatened by anything you may think, feel, or experience. You are bathed in the knowing that, in fact, nothing truly exists but the support of Source.

ATTUNEMENT
Feeling the Support of Source

1. Periodically take time to sit quietly and let your breath take you to your inner Source. With each breath, gently think or speak your intention to connect. You may use words such as, "I align with the unwavering support of Source that is always with me" or "I open to the support of Source." Let yourself feel the supportive presence of Source. If your mind wanders, simply repeat your affirmation of intent. Enjoy the connection.

2. Take a walk or jog and allow the movement of your body and the beauty of nature to bring your awareness to your inner Source. As you move, occasionally use a verbal affirmation, such as the ones mentioned above, to direct your intention and keep you on purpose.

3. Talk about your inner Source of support with other people. When you are in touch with it, or would like to be, talking about what Source feels like and how you draw on its support can be a form of meditation. If this talk is not done as idle chatter but is used to take you into the experience, it can make the inner connection more real. Choose to do your sharing with people, perhaps good friends or a spiritual

support group, who can understand and who also want a deep experience of Source.

49

Personality as Ally

One theme that has emerged so far in this book is that the personality habitually overlooks or rejects unlimited spirit. As the inner navigator who knows how to get us through limited reality, personality seems to have little ability to recognize unlimitedness. Instead, it works hard to stay in control of what it knows. When unlimitedness is experienced, personality often interprets it as a disruption. Its automatic reaction, then, is to try to put an end to the disruption so it may return to what is familiar. In this way, personality resists unlimitedness.

Fortunately, there is also another side to this story, a side in which personality longs for unlimitedness. Because personality is the aspect of our being that experiences separation from Source, it is the aspect of our being in which all suffering takes place. Yet, personality truly does *not* like to suffer.

Even if suffering is a long-established, habituated pattern in your life that seems impossible to break, your personality still does not like it. Perhaps you were given the impression in childhood that you are most "real" when you are suffering; or that you are living in the most righteous way when you are in pain; or that people will be kinder or less rejecting if you are suffering. This can cause your personality to cling to suffering as a self-affirming reality. Still, even underneath that ingrained pattern, your personality longs to be free from suffering and to heal.

When you allow unlimitedness into your conscious awareness enough times, your personality begins to recognize that unlimitedness *is* a possibility. As this exposure continues, your personality becomes willing to support your intention to live without limitation rather than resist. It then begins to stretch, opening to the greater reality in spite of old attachments and beliefs in limitation. Such a turning point is significant.

Look for those times in your life when there is resistance to unlimitedness. For example, when you are experiencing more of true self's well-being in your life, your personality may pipe up and say, "This is not real. You are a fool to create your life around unlimited thinking or unlimited action. Who do you think you are, anyway? And what makes you think any of this new stuff will work?" In those comments you are hearing your personality's fear and need for control. Recognize the fear and control, and give them a blessing. You do not need to resist them, for it does not help you to resist your resistance. You simply need to feel the distress it causes. Notice the pain that creeps in with not trusting your true self.

As you recognize this discomfort and get to know it, you can say, "Yes, here it is again." With that acceptance you are open enough to also add, "In the midst of this distress in my personality, I choose to open to true self. I long for well-being, and I am willing to receive it. I let unlimited love and well-being fill my body. I allow myself to be a conduit for vibrant life force."

This kind of affirmation of your truest intent has tremendous power. Remember that regardless of whether you feel the transformation in that moment, something important happens from that inner statement. Use whatever image or words seem the most natural for you. The form of your affirmation is important only to capture your intent; your intent is what will activate the transformation.

50

Bridging the Split

We have talked about the split as the gap that appears to exist between limitation and unlimitedness in our lives. The split can be perceived in many ways, including our difficulty in creating tangible outer conditions or events that reflect our inner expanded awareness. As long as we experience limitation and unlimitedness as separate rather than integrated, the split will continue to seem real.

We have also discussed the importance of not trying to escape or reject the split and have looked at ways to make use of the power that lies hidden within it. Understand, however, that you are not destined to stay in the split forever. The steps you take in exploring the split are meant to take you to a bridge where you can complete your crossing. Or, more accurately, those steps are meant to take you into *being* the bridge that brings your inner transcendent experience into outer manifestation in your world.

The bridge can be found, ironically, in the very aspect of your being that creates the split in the first place: your personality. Its experience of separation is what keeps the split in existence. As your personality accepts unlimitedness into its awareness and belief system, its reality begins to change. It increasingly experiences itself as part of the greater whole rather than as separate. As your personality's reality shifts to include this unity, the split narrows and unlimitedness begins to be expressed in your manifestations in the outer world.

The personality takes on a new role
as it finds its true power in being
the loyal servant to unlimited spirit.

You may notice this shift as a lessening of the gap between your personality's daily reality and your occasions of expanded awareness. You no longer have the sense of needing to give up expanded awareness to function in the limited world, nor do you have to give up personality's daily concerns to live with expanded awareness. The two realities become integrated within you, and that integration starts appearing in your external manifestations. There is more room for you to be all of who you are—everywhere!

Because personality is oriented to physical reality and is adept at functioning in limitation, it knows about manifesting in the physical world. Your frustration in the past was, in fact, that most of your manifestations seemed straight from your personality and were, therefore, too limiting for the part of you that was growing. Your personality can manifest only what it experiences. If it experiences only limitation, that is what it manifests in your outer life.

When your personality is integrated with unlimited awareness and identifies it as "real", it is able to outwardly manifest that unlimitedness. Then you are able to see outer change in your life that reflects your inner transformation. Whatever you have been seeking—whether satisfying work, relationship, or another situation for expressing your true self in the world—is created naturally and appropriately.

This is one area in which having a strong and healthy personality pays off. The clearer and more balanced your personality is, and the more adept it is at functioning in the physical world, the better it can blend unlimitedness into the forms it creates in your life.

A healthy personality that has opened its consciousness to unlimitedness becomes a strong vehicle for conveying true self's expanded perspective and unlimited well-being into your daily life. It can maintain balance and awareness of true self while taking action in the world. Similarly, it will be able to speak or write and consciously express true self through that communication. And one of its great joys will be recognizing the reflection of unlimited spirit in situations that once seemed filled with limitation.

51

Approaching the Bridge

Just before reaching the bridge of integration, there is a gate. Standing in front of the gate can seem almost like torture. You are impatient and want to cross the bridge. You stand on one foot and then on the other, waiting for the gate to open. You can see where you want to be and can even imagine what it would be like to have a life that reflects unlimitedness. True self is becoming more real and limitation more unbearable. Still, the gate does not let you pass.

The most empowering thing you can do while you wait at the gate is to be fully present right where you are. It may be tempting to mentally project yourself across to the other side, by either wondering why you aren't already there or convincing yourself that you are. Letting yourself imagine the new reality can help prepare you for creating it in your life, but mentally escaping into the new reality to avoid being where you are is a form of self-rejection and will only delay your progress.

All true change is made in a state of self-acceptance.

You will open the gate by accepting where you are. As you face the gate, you have tremendous power you may not even realize. *You have the power to accept limitation.* This may sound disappointing, and your response may be, "But I don't want to accept limitation; I want to get away from it!"

Consider two things. First, notice that the description given in "Bridging the Split" about the fully integrated state *included* limitation. But when you become the bridge, you will not be caught in the limitation—you will be able to carry the limited and unlimited *together.* You cannot carry what you resist, so to become the bridge you must be without resistance to either. If you are still trying to escape limitation, you are resisting it and are not ready for the integration.

Second, recognize that accepting limitation does not mean you have to be comfortable with it. You can accept yourself and still not always feel comfortable with yourself. You can accept fear and not necessarily be comfortable with situations where you are afraid. So, you can accept limitation and not be entirely comfortable with it. What is significant about acceptance, however, is that as you witness your discomfort, you sense that at your core you are in well-being. Even if your emotions and your nervous system seem to be struggling with the situation, your inner witness is in well-being and you recognize it as the greater power. This distinction is important.

The willingness to carry the paradox
of well-being within distress is the
ability to hold power.

If you are still facing the gate, you are still developing your ability to hold power and to carry it into your life. After you move through the gate, you will definitely need this ability, so it is with compassionate wisdom that your greater self has you stand on this side of the gate until you are ready for it to open.

The best practice for carrying power is to give yourself extended periods of true well-being and connection with Source. That is the power that will ultimately be streaming through your being into your life, uniting you with the infinite possibilities you now hold in your heart.

52

Carrying Power

Power comes from *consciously* being unlimited. You are unlimited already and always have been. Sustained conscious awareness of your unlimitedness is all that is really needed to make a dramatic difference in your life. With that change, you embody true well-being regardless of whether you are in a situation that is comfortable or uncomfortable, "positive" or "negative". Nothing can separate you from Source.

While you stand at the gate gathering power your system is learning to carry greater and greater well-being. As you choose to align with Source in the midst of all thought, all feeling, and all situations, you are teaching your body about the presence of true self.

It may seem strange that your body needs to learn this presence, but it does. Your body's circuitry has been laid out largely according to your personality's experience of limitation. As you become more aligned with true self, and as the well-being of Source begins to fill more of your physical body, your body's pathways of consciousness are repatterned. It is as though the conduits once were meant to hold a smaller reality, and now they are expanding to carry an unlimited one.

Imagine that even the tissues of your body are being taught something new. Every cell has programmed within it not only its physical function, but also an ability to experience consciousness. Each cell in your body has some experience of the consciousness of the whole organism that you are. As the inner circuitry grows in unlimitedness, the cells are, in a sense, reprogrammed with a greater consciousness and, therefore, a greater vitality. The physical tissues are infused with more vibrant well-being and potential for a healthier, extended life.

53
Discharging Excess Energy

It can be uncomfortable to increase well-being in your body if your circuits are not used to it. It may take time for the inner adjustments to occur that will establish equilibrium around the increase of vibrancy you carry. If being so highly charged is something you are not used to, your body may feel the impulse to discharge some of the energy. It is all right to do this; after your body has received the increased charge, it will use the full imprint as the model for expanding its energetic circuitry. That imprint will remain and will be used by your body long after you discharge the energy that feels like excess.

How you release this energy is important and requires your making some conscious choices. Let's explore some possibilities. At the top of the list of appropriate outlets is physical exercise. Of course, it should be exercise that is beneficial to your body and its condition, and preferably something you enjoy doing. In exercise you are discharging a buildup of vibrant life force through an activity that is also physically strengthening to your body and, therefore, to your personality. It supports your total well-being and directly increases your ability to carry power in the future.

What if you do not wish to exercise or you have a physical condition that does not permit it? Life is unlimited; you always have an alternative.

Your imagination is a good resource. Imagining is easy and can be done along with or instead of physical exercise. For example, when you feel the buildup of intense vibration and the need for discharge, take five to twenty minutes for the following inner process.

―――――――――― ――――――――――

ATTUNEMENT
Discharging Excess Energy

1. Imagine your body bathed from head to toe in vitality. . . . Your tissues receive this vitality as spiritual nutrients, and your cells glow with life. . . .

2. As your body is energized by this vitality, it intuitively knows how much energy it needs to keep and how much it needs to release. Imagine that your body releases the right amount through the pores of your skin. Like light shining through a porous cloth, this extra vitality illuminates the space around you and is then released into your life. . . .

3. To close, spend at least one minute allowing your body to feel a comfortable sense of well-being and ease. . . .

―――――――――― ――――――――――

Feel free to experiment with different images. Sometimes you may find that the energy wants to leave through certain areas of your body, or you may be inclined to breathe the energy out with each exhale.

When excess energy is released, it is not "gotten rid of" because of anything being wrong with it. There is nothing wrong with it; it is vitality from Source. It would not have been within you to begin with if it did not have something good to give you. As you release this energy it goes to work for you. It knows, by its own intelligence, where to go in your life, how to guide you, and what to manifest—without your having to give it any further thought! Just releasing your excess energy sets this all in motion.

Be creative finding other ways of energetic discharge that work for you. A hot bath may help, a quiet walk in the woods, or five minutes imagining you are running through the surf at the beach. Housecleaning, gardening, or even reading the funnies can be good. Phoning a friend who understands your process and giving a "vibrancy report" is an excellent way to feel the energy and discharge it through talking about it.

Recognizing when you need to discharge excess vibrancy and consciously choosing a self-nurturing way to do it can stop you from falling into a pattern of unconscious behavior that weakens your system rather than strengthens it. When excess energy is not discharged, any discomfort you feel from increased vitality may prompt you automatically and unconsciously to numb, distract, or subdue yourself.

You may do this by drinking coffee, over- or under-eating, snacking on sugary foods, over- or under-exercising, escaping into mental activity, watching TV, surfing the internet, over-focusing on a relationship, using drugs or alcohol, or turning to other types of addictive or potentially self-destructive behavior.

So as you open to new levels of vibrancy, be aware of whether it is at all uncomfortable for you. Take responsibility for creating rituals that allow you to receive vibrant well-being, to direct it, and to release excess energy into your life. This is vibrancy management and is your secret for carrying power.

54

Moving Through the Gate

Your acceptance of limitation and familiarity with well-being open the gate; then your ability to identify with the unlimited will move you through it. You cannot force or control your movement through the gate any more than you could have forced the gate open or could have flung yourself across the split. Making the shift from identifying with the limitation in your thoughts and experiences to identifying with the unlimited is what propels you forward.

Why is it necessary to accept limitation to stop identifying with it? You identify with everything you resist. To stop identifying with limitation, you must stop resisting it. When you do stop identifying with limitation you still experience it, but is no longer a barrier for you. It becomes just another of life's explorations. You no longer hold onto it and it no longer stops you from being and expressing who you truly are.

Moving through the gate and becoming the bridge changes your life in tangible ways. For example, if you have been struggling to find work that allows you to relate to the world from the expanded awareness of your true self, that work will manifest. If you have been looking for a relationship that supports you in being all of who you truly are, you will find your partner. If you have longed for outer abundance that reflects the abundance and well-being that has begun to grow within you, you will find that, too. The list of possibilities is endless.

What manifests for you in the world
comes directly from your sense of self.

To the degree you identify with limitation, you carry it in your sense of self. Therefore, that limitation manifests into your world. As you identify less with limitation, your outer manifestations reflect less limitation. Similarly, as you identify more with unlimitedness, you carry unlimitedness in your sense of self and that unlimitedness manifests. You then live with more situations that recognizably reflect unlimited being and support your expanded awareness.

Understand that identifying with unlimitedness or limitation is not the same as indentifying with what is "positive" or "negative". It is the limited aspect of the personality that thinks in terms of "positive" and "negative". To guide you through that reality, personality may tell you that you should think more positive thoughts or relate only to positive experiences if you want to live in a positive world.

The hidden, self-defeating message in this belief is that anything perceived as negative is potentially dangerous. That creates a need to avoid, deny, or resist the negative by continually turning to the positive—

which actually keeps you identified with the negative because it is your frame of reference. If you are content to remain at your personality's level of limitation, avoiding negativity may seem appropriate. But if you intend to expand your awareness of yourself, others, and the world beyond the narrow confines of identification with limitation, you will need to recognize that nothing is innately positive or negative.

Positive and negative are simply personality's translation of comfortable and uncomfortable, trusted and not trusted. Yet Source, the vitality of life and brilliance of all creation, is the core energy of all things and all beings—as well as all thoughts, feelings, and situations. At that essence level, how can anything be innately negative? With unlimited love and unwavering well-being as the essence energy that *everything*, including your pleasant and unpleasant experiences, is made of—where is there true negativity?

You can afford to be all embracing.

It can be helpful to notice when something seems pleasant or unpleasant to you, comfortable or uncomfortable, safe or unsafe, life enhancing or depleting. Use that information to make your choices. That is part of honoring your personality's needs and is at times necessary for protecting yourself or supporting your emotional and physical health. Yet, you work against your movement into greater awareness if you reject or resist all thoughts, feelings, and life situations that your personality perceives as negative. It may serve you to look beyond the discomfort and "negativity" and connect with Source, which is at the core of all of it.

MEDITATION
Moving Through the Gate

1. Breathe gently and easily, allowing each breath to take you just a little deeper into your true self. . . .

2. As your breath takes you a little deeper and a little deeper into true self, it is also taking you into well-being. . . . You do not need to try to create this well-being or do anything to make it stronger. Unlimited well-being is already within you, no matter how subtle it feels, and your breath gently and easily takes you to it. . . .

3. The gate through which you will be passing is in this well-being. As you move into your true self and into the well-being, you find the gate. . . . As you stand in front of the gate, it opens for you. . . .

4. To move through the gate, draw on Source energy (true self) in the midst of all your thoughts, emotions, and physical sensations as they arise. . . . That energy—it's vibrant life, unconditional love, and unlimited well-being—may be very subtle, but it is real. Let yourself enjoy it.

5. If you feel any excess energy in your system, let it be released through the pores of your skin into the world. . . .

6. To close, let your body be bathed with a feeling of comfort and relaxation. Then stretch and open your eyes.

55
The Nothing

After making the shift to a new level of consciousness, you may be surprised to find yourself feeling disoriented, as though you can't see the terrain and get your bearings. You may think, "This isn't what I thought it would be." Of course it isn't—you had imagined it from your old level of conscious awareness, which was more limited. You have stepped into your greater potential, which is a more subtle realm. Until your conscious awareness acclimates to this subtlety, you may be facing the Nothing.

People usually think the Nothing means something is wrong. For example, when I guide people into true self, they sometimes say disappointedly, "I'm not getting anything. There's nothing there." That is music to my ears. It confirms they are dipping deeper into their true self than they are used to. Their impulse is to reject the experience and give up or do something else. But the thing to do is to *stay right there*. Just hang out. Be. Hover at the edge of the Nothing. Be gently curious and wait.

The deeper you go into true self, the more subtle the experience.

No matter your current level of conscious awareness, the Nothing is always the next level deeper—and reality there, including all sensations, is more subtle than you are used to perceiving. As long as your conscious awareness is still oriented to the previous, denser level and hasn't yet acclimated to the new subtlety, it will not perceive deeper reality. It will think nothing is there! Yet, if you calmly let your conscious awareness hover in the Nothing, it will automatically acclimate and begin to perceive what previously it could not. That is how awareness expands.

You already trust your physical perception to do this. If you step from a brightly lit room into a room so dimly lit that it seems completely dark, what will happen if you just stand there awhile? Your eyes will adapt, of course. Within a few minutes you will begin to make out shapes of the furniture, perhaps starting with the couch and large chairs. The longer you stand there, the clearer the room will become.

This is exactly how it works with the Nothing. As you patiently wait in the Nothing, your conscious awareness will adjust to the new subtlety and begin to perceive it. A deeper reality based in greater love, wisdom and true self well-being will appear. *But it will be subtle.* You must be willing to value experience so subtle that at first you are not even sure it is real. For example, you may notice a feeling of calm and well-being so tiny that previously you would have overlooked it in your expectation of a stronger sensation. Or microscopic self-love may waft so gently through your chest that you previously would have thought it didn't count.

The longer you wait in the Nothing, the more will be revealed—and the more real it will become to you. The more frequently you return to the Nothing, the easier and more natural the transition will become. With each visit to the Nothing your conscious awareness will learn to expand.

MEDITATION
Being in the Nothing

1. Breathe gently and easily, allowing each breath to take you just a little deeper into your true self. . . .

2. Assume that each breath will continue taking you a little deeper into true self, even when you are not thinking of it.

3. As you breathe, be gently curious about finding a place in your body where you feel nothing. If tensions or aches call to you, or you feel specific emotions or notice a flurry of thoughts, do not push them away. Just let them be in the background; they are not what interests you right now. Be gently drawn to a place where there seems to be nothing happening.

4. Let your awareness hover at that place of no sensation as you breathe.

5. If sensations arise in that place, do not push them away. Just let them be in the background; they are not what interests you right now. Continue letting your awareness be drawn to the Nothing in your body, even if it's in a new place, and gently hover.

6. When you become comfortable with the Nothing, add this element: Gently look for the tiniest, most microscopic well-being you can find, and let your awareness hover in it.

7. If that well-being grows or changes, again gently look for the tiniest, most microscopic well-being you can find, and let your awareness hover in it. . . and so on. . . .

8. To close, let your body be bathed with a feeling of comfort and relaxation. Then stretch, open your eyes, and move slowly.

encountering a block in myself. For weeks, every time I meditated I was confronted with the same dark, empty nothingness.

"I went to one of your talks and asked you about it. In your true self channeling, you told me, 'Go into that darkness and emptiness. The Nothing isn't really empty. *Everything* is there. Even the stars are there. The universe is there for you.'

"At that point everything changed. I realized that the darkness wasn't really nothing; I just wasn't seeing what was there yet. Understanding was a relief to me. I decided then and there to open to the new level of awareness that was presenting itself to me as The Nothing. I started believing, 'I'm not doing anything wrong. I'm supposed to be here with the nothingness. Darkness is just what it looks like to me now; I need to move into it.'

"In my next meditation the dark hole of nothingness appeared again, and I opened my mind by asking, 'What else is here that I haven't noticed? What else is coming to me here?' I thought of the stars, and then everything started moving. Stars whooshed by, and new ideas and awareness flowed through me, showing me more of my true self and how expansive I am in my being. Then I was moving with the stars; I was part of them. Whatever they were, I had the same stuff in me. I had all potential.

"It changed my life to experience that I really am part of the universe. I am not separate from it. I am not a stranger in it after all. I am part of the whole."

"Did you used to feel separate?" I asked.

"Oh, yes, definitely. For as long as I can remember I had felt that I didn't really belong here, in this world, on earth. Before opening to The Nothing, I used to look out my window at the trees on the hillside and think, 'There's a world out there, and I'm not part of it.' It felt sad, but normal.

"Then one day, after I had started moving into The Nothing in my meditations, I was looking out my window at the trees on the hillside, as usual, but this time it felt different. Instead of looking *at* them and feeling separate, I felt I was part of them. I felt connected. It made me stop and think, 'I'm looking out at the world, and I feel that I belong here. I've never felt this way before. Wow, I've really changed how I perceive myself and my place in the world—and my place in the universe.' My old belief about not belonging had shifted.

"That shift had a profound effect on my life. Because of it, I carried forward a knowing that I really *do* belong here, I *am* a part of life, and the universe *wants* me here. Now, 20 years later, I still carry that knowing; I can feel it in the cells of my body. I know that I'll never go back to feeling like I don't belong in this world."

"How did that knowing stay with you?" I asked in awe. I had noticed over the years that Louisa was facile at getting back in touch with true self whenever the stresses of life pulled her off track. "Did you do anything to keep renewing the knowing, or did it just stay with you on its own?"

"Practice, practice, practice! I've practiced staying in touch with it, by choice. My expansiveness, my connection with the universe, and my belonging in the world have stayed real to me because I've made a point of integrating them into my daily life. I practiced a lot!"

"How did you do that?" I asked.

"First, I continued to meditate. I recognized that the expansive experience in my meditations was not just an 'altered state.' It was a reality, a legitimate and important reality. I chose to accept it as a reality, a normal part of my life here on earth, and to value it.

"Second, at the end of every meditation, I chose to integrate my expansive experience from that meditation into my daily awareness. For awhile, although I had accepted my expansive experience as a reality, it seemed like a separate reality that didn't connect with my daily reality— being at work, talking with people, driving, shopping, fixing dinner, and so on.

"So I added a third step: At various times during my daily activities, I made a point of pausing to remember my expansive experience and to invite it into my day. Especially helpful was the image of the stars from my meditation. To me, it represented my being part of the unlimited universe and, simultaneously, belonging in this world. Remembering the stars brought my true self into my personality in an instant.

"Cultivating the integration took a lot of practice, and doing it felt like exercise—like I was exercising my awareness muscles. But it was worth it. Because I kept repeating those exercises, my two worlds started to blend. My expansive state from meditation, which was my true self, and my daily awareness, which was my personality, began integrating. That integration has continued over the years."

"Was this all done with your awareness, or did you do something tangible, too?" I asked.

"I got creative about giving myself tangible reminders so I wouldn't get caught up in my day and forget, especially at work where distractions were greatest. Some days I would put a short, inspiring quote on my desk and read it every couple of hours. Reading the quote would trigger my expanded awareness in the midst of the hubbub of work. Other days I would light a candle on my desk to remind my subconscious, whenever I looked in that direction, that my true self had come to work with me. Or I would put a special, little stone in my pocket when I got dressed in the morning. During the day I would notice it whenever I put my hand in my pocket, or sometimes I would just remember it was there, and that would remind me to take a breath and open to my true self.

"Over the years, I've also used the big challenges in my life as opportunities for integrating my true self and personality. Those were the times I needed it most, anyway."

Louisa stopped, thinking she was done with her story. "Hey, keep talking. This is fabulous. Give me some examples," I told her.

"Okay. Let's see...oh, yes, money and relationship. The real biggies. Money, or my lack of it, used to seem like an insurmountable obstacle to my happiness. Back then, thinking of money made me feel, 'I can't be part of life because I don't have money. I'm not like everybody else. I don't belong. I don't deserve to be here.' Not having money made me feel weak, not entitled to goodness, and different from everybody else.

"It seemed to me that everybody else was able to live life in a fully engaged way, but I could not. Everybody else was in a big, colorful parade, complete with bands, balloons and floats, trumpeting its way down the street, but I couldn't be in it. I was on the curb watching it all go by.

"I had been living with that perspective for so long that I had no awareness of it or how it was affecting me until my therapist pointed it out. She helped me to notice how I felt about myself and money—and then she helped me to realize that those limiting beliefs weren't true. That got me jump started.

"From there, I started applying my spiritual 'exercises' to money. When I thought of money, I made a point of remembering the stars from meditation. When the old feelings of unworthiness and not belonging because I had money struggles sneaked back in, I did the exercise again: taking a few breaths and remembering the stars and my expansiveness. Or sometimes I looked out the window for 10 seconds and remembered, 'I *am* a part of things.' When I caught myself having that feeling of being on the curb as everybody else's parade passed by me, I just reminded myself, 'That's not true,' and the feeling lost its power. Practice, practice, practice!"

"And the exercises helped?" I asked.

"Doing those exercises made a world of difference! I felt a new lightness come over me. My old associations with money—feelings of shame, not deserving, and not belonging—transformed to feelings of belonging, being part of the universe, and being part of life. Experiencing myself as an integral (and wanted!) part of life made me increasingly feel that I deserved all goodness, including money.

"I made this integration of true self into my personality's experience in tiny steps over the years. And I'm so glad I did it! Now that I feel I'm a part of the movement and flow of the universe, and that money connects rather than separates me from it, my whole life moves and flows. My life is full, like the universe is full.

"In retrospect, it's clear that feeling a part of the universe made me feel more supported, and as I integrated that feeling of universal support into my thoughts and feelings about money, my finances grew to support me in this world. Career opportunities improved, and my income increased. These days my finances are balanced, and I feel comfortable."

"And relationship?" I asked. We had hashed over our relationships for years, so I was curious to hear her perspective now.

"The tough thing for me in relationship was that I would easily lose my sense of self, my rootedness in who I am. I would adapt to the man too much, without even knowing it, until I lost my self-esteem and self-confidence. His wants and needs would become more important than my own. At that point it would be hard for me to get my authentic self back because I felt small, like I didn't deserve much, and reclaiming myself felt like trudging upstream, against the current of the man's expectations of me.

"This was especially true with my last boyfriend, who, as you know, was very overpowering. Finally I decided to take a stand for myself. I made the commitment to be grounded and balanced. I created a mental exercise in which I said to myself, 'I'm going to stand my ground. I'm going to be who I am. Who I am is good. It does not matter what he thinks, how he criticizes me, or how much he rants and raves at me. I will remain loyal to my authentic self.'

"By that time, I already had developed my strong experience of true self. My expanded awareness in meditation had begun to help me with money, so I called on that expanded awareness to help me in relationship, too. It reminded me, 'I am who I am. I am in the universe, and the universe is in me. I am the stars, and the stars are me. I belong in this world, and I am wanted here.' Remembering that truth gave me confidence in who I was as a whole being. Because of it, I realized that even if I had flaws, I was much more than my flaws.

"It wasn't always easy, but I became increasingly authentic in the relationship, expressing more of my wants and needs. I got many backlashes from my boyfriend, so I turned to the support of good friends and my therapist for help remembering who I was and what I wanted. Finally he and I broke up because it became clear that he wanted a relationship with the 'lesser' me rather than the real me. It was painful for me to lose the fantasy that we were going to be good together someday, but it was better to find out the truth and move on. Since then, knowing that I am as big, expansive, and powerful as the universe has kept me from losing myself to another person or handing over my self esteem.

"I'm not in a relationship right now, but as I look at my life, I can tell you that it genuinely reflects me. The well-being, contentment, belonging, and love of life I feel, plus my work and house, all feel like they reflect me. It all has come as a direct result of moving into The Nothing, integrating my expanded awareness into my daily life, allowing myself to be who I authentically am, and understanding that I am a reflection of all that is true in the universe.

"I still have struggles sometimes, and I do my spiritual 'exercises' when I need them. I know this for sure: My integration of true self's expanded awareness into my life has brought me abundance and profound contentment."

Part X

PLANETARY SURVIVAL

Facing Challenge in the World

56
Deepening Your Awareness

Your breath has intelligence; it can guide your awareness into true self the moment you ask it to. You can draw on this intelligence right now. For the next few moments, notice your breathing and imagine that you are allowing each breath to take you into true self. Only a slight change is necessary; you are closer to true self than you think. Let the next breath take you just a little deeper. . . . And the next breath a little deeper still. . . . And the next breath. . . .

When you start your day with a few minutes of presence in true self and return to it periodically as the day progresses, you change the quality of your life. You operate from a new inner depth and, therefore, relate to a deeper level of everyone and everything around you. At the end of the day, even though you may have gone through the normal course of events and have had your usual responses, something will be different. The world will have left a new imprint on you and, whether you noticed it or not, you will have had a new effect on people.

Living from even a slightly deeper place within yourself
expands your perceptions of the world around you
and enriches your interactions with other people.

This does not necessarily mean that you will be calm or happy all the time, that people will do what you want them to do, or that nothing will bother you anymore. It does not even mean that the events in your life will occur any differently. It is the quality of your life that will transform. You will become more fully present, closer to a state of well-being that remains constant regardless of any fluctuations in emotions or circumstances. You will become more centered in true self.

This transformation matters because you are part of a planetary shift in consciousness, a consistent worldwide progression into deeper, more expansive levels of self. The world you experience in ten or twenty years will be very different from the one you experience today. You are part of this world, intimately connected to everyone in it; the greater awareness you develop in your life is your personal contribution to planetary growth.

57
Survival and the One Mind

In spite of the spiritual transformation taking place, thinking about what the world may be like in ten or twenty years can be disquieting. The current crises on the planet include widespread problems relating to the environment, economic instability, societal violence, wars, starvation, health, human rights, and the dangers of atomic power and weaponry. Clearly the path we are following needs some major repair work if we expect it to take us into a healthy future.

Many people who are spiritually focused relate to these crises with fear and panic. "We must hurry and evolve or we will not survive!" This is a contradiction: belief in the power of spiritual evolution and fear for survival. Spiritual evolution is a given; there is no need to fear that it will not happen or that it will not happen fast enough.

The human species and the planet
will survive and thrive.

Throughout human existence, people have always had reasons to be concerned for their survival. What makes current survival issues particularly significant is that they are no longer limited to individual, personal concerns ("Will my self/family/country survive?"), but now extend to fears and deep caring about the condition of the entire planet. This is logical because we know we now have the power to destroy life on that great a scale. And along with the development of this destructive power have come the iconic photos of planet Earth taken from space, tangible proof that we are one population sharing one home, undeniably interconnected and interdependent.

The result of the recognition of our united existence and our united vulnerability is that individuals can no longer struggle solely on their own in an isolated way, with their personal issues of survival. Because survival of the world now is at stake, it is necessary for all people to become aware of their effect on the planetary whole. And from there it must go a step deeper still.

The group mind, the consciousness
shared by all beings on earth,
must become real to us.

Let's step back for a moment and review this from the broader perspective. Unlimited love is the essence of our being. It is the building material for all forms of life and all events that occur everywhere on earth. As the Source of all creation and existence, unlimited love is what is most real. It is also what is most enduring; it cannot be destroyed. The forms of its expression can be changed—from water to steam, fire to smoke, a sky scraper to rubble, a fetus to a newborn, one thought or emotion to another—but the unlimited love and creative intelligence of vibrant life force cannot be harmed. It knows only joy, the joy of being.

Consider that unlimited Source does not fear for its survival. Because it recognizes all things as creative manifestations of its love, it is not afraid of anything. It never forgets that what is most real is the love and vibrant life force at the core of everything.

Being fully aware of itself, unlimited Source notices that the expression of itself called "the human personality" believes in fear and a limited view of life. Yet the personality longs to evolve beyond the constraints and suffering of its limited reality into the expansive well-being of unlimited life, and this creates a pull on Source to assist. Source's assistance comes through events that allow the personality to grow on its own terms, involving issues the personality recognizes as real.

The personality's most fundamental concern is its survival. Because it experiences itself as more real than unlimited spirit, it fears the loss of itself more than anything. It wants to preserve its way of organizing the world around itself, and is resistant to any drastic change. This means that survival issues get the personality's full attention the moment they arise.

With support from the greater consciousness of Source, we all have created the planetary crises to assist the personality in recognizing the oneness we all share. Our physical survival now depends on the world's people coming together with one mind, one intent, one purpose: to find values and actions that nurture the earth and its residents.

Your greatest personal contribution to the survival—and *thrival*—of the planet can be made by becoming aware of the connection you already share with all beings on the planet. There is nothing you have to do spiritually to unite with others, for that union has already occurred; just by existing you are naturally in One mind. One mind is a quality of spirit emanating from Source; it is the thought and creativity shared by all beings. What now matters most is directing your conscious awareness to this connection.

Understand that being in One mind does not mean that everyone thinks the same thoughts; it is not a mass joining of the personality's intellect. Nor does it mean that you lose any of your autonomy. You will continue to be the full individual you have always been. One mind is simply an interconnectedness in spirit that transcends the personality's experience of separation and limitation.

One mind is the spiritual intelligence
shared by all beings.

As you become aware of your participation in One mind, you open the door for expansive thought to come into your conscious daily life where it can be put to practical use. You are essentially reaching into a realm in which all possibilities are held in "potential", inviting them to move through you into "real life". Naturally, this broadens the range of information and creative impulse you draw from as you create your life and make your contribution to planetary transformation.

This expansion will come as you regularly witness your unity with all beings. You can practice this witnessing through meditations like the one at the end of this chapter or by simply imagining unity from time to time during the day. As your natural place in One mind becomes real to you, your personality will be able to receive and use the greater perspective and creativity that is shared in unity. This connection will bring a subtle, new power to your thoughts, ideas, and actions.

In One mind, you are sharing
a limitless resource of thought
with all beings on the planet.

One mind is a collective pool of thought, which means that everyone draws from it. This resource is not made up of specific ideas so it is not limited to, or even influenced by, the human intellect. It is pure thought. It is the source of all ideas, yet it is infinitely more than ideas.

In other words, One mind is not a network through which everyone exchanges ideas. Getting an idea is not a matter of reaching into this reservoir and pulling out a thought that suits you. Instead, the vibrant energy of unlimited thought always moves through you. Your brain translates the energy of pure thought into your personal thoughts, doing so according to your sense of reality. The *essence* energy of those ideas comes from One mind: your connection with all beings and all possibility.

You may know other people whose ideas are similar to yours. There are always groups of people translating the unlimited vibration of thought in similar ways. Yet each idea shared by the group still begins in the personal identity of each individual. The idea itself is not any more real than that. What is real—before, during, and after the life of the idea—is the vibrant energy of unlimited thought.

This relates directly to the transition of the planetary consciousness. Your contact with true self will attune your awareness to a more refined vibration, a different frequency than you identify with now. It will enable your brain to interpret the energy patterns of pure thought in ways that it cannot presently do. You will translate thought into ideas that, at this moment, seem beyond you because you are not yet consciously connected with true self at such a deep level.

The profound ideas that will contribute to the thrival of the planet will come from a refinement in the translation of unlimited thought into ideas. As you move deeper into true self in your daily life, you assist this process of evolution. The deepening of your conscious connection with true self and One mind will increase your ability to hold awareness at a more refined vibrational frequency. And the energy patterning of your new sense of self will manifest as more expansive thoughts, actions, and life experiences.

Recognize the contribution this allows you to make to the world. Perhaps your way of working for a more harmonious planet includes, or even centers on, political activity or making changes in your lifestyle. Yet even in the midst of your life-enhancing practical action, the most powerful thing you can do is to continue to contact deeper levels of self. This will give your actions greater effect and will provide you with the necessary attunement to bring creative, new solutions to the world.

MEDITATION
The One Mind

1. As you breathe, imagine that each breath has a natural intelligence that knows your true self and gently takes you there.

2. As your breath keeps breathing you deeper into true self, let your imagination show you your connection to the group consciousness—the One mind of all beings on the planet. . . . The One mind is a vibrant pulse of life that carries unlimited love and unlimited thought directly to you.

3. Notice that this vibrant essence of unlimited love and unlimited thought is greater than the personal you, yet your mind translates it into ideas and perceptions that create your experience of the world. . . .

4. The energy of thought moves through your being and is then released to become unlimited, unformed thought once more. . . . Continue to witness the One mind as it enters you, is translated into your world, then flows on to become the unlimited One mind again. . . .

5. As you continue receiving the One mind, notice the unlimited love it circulates through you. With each breath, allow your body to feel the joy of having this subtle love move into your tissues. . . .

6. Imagine that this love radiates through your body and out the pores of your skin, directly into your personal world, the world you live in every day. . . .Unlimited love goes into everything in your environment. It goes into the metal of your car, into the material of your home, into the clothes in your closet. . . .

7. Slowly open your eyes and look around. Be aware that this emanation of love and unlimited thought continues as you go about your life. . . . You have witnessed your connection with the One mind. You have allowed it to touch you, to become more real to you, and to come into your conscious life.

58
Transforming Fear

We live in a time when the personality's survival issues are being globally stimulated, and fear about personal safety and the possible ruin of the planet is at an all-time high. Some frightened people point to past, present, and future-predicted disasters, caused by humans or by nature, and declare those disasters to be evidence of how close the planet is to destruction.

Fear is beneficial to the extent it prompts you to take notice of the circumstances you are living with and motivates you to take constructive action. It can be a healthy wake-up call, releasing enough adrenaline into your system to help you move through old patterns of denial or inaction. But if fear is overwhelming you and causing you to shut down or to identify with the doom, something is amiss. You are caught in a closed circuit in which fear is working against you rather than for you.

> *Crisis is meant to be identified,*
> *not identified with.*

Remember, you manifest what you carry in your experience of self, especially the issues you identify with or believe to be most real. As you identify with fear and disaster, the energy patterns of that identity emanate into your world and take form, perpetuating the very distress that already overwhelms you.

This does not mean you should resist your fear (or other feelings) or that you should ignore distress in the world to prevent manifesting more of it. You do not manifest everything you feel or observe or respond to, but rather only what you carry in your identity. In fact, refusing to allow certain feelings or look at specific issues will not keep you from identifying with them; it will just keep you out of touch with what you are carrying.

So what can you do when you hear about disasters, present or predicted, from people who are in a state of fear? These four steps may help you make constructive use of what can be an overwhelming cultural input of frightening information.

ATTUNEMENT
Responding to People's Fear

1. Be aware of the fear those people are projecting. Then notice where that fear resonates in yourself. Survival fears may center on your basic human needs such as having enough money or a loving relationship. Or, you may be afraid for your physical survival or for the survival of the whole planet. Notice the kind of fear you are feeling, and then acknowledge it as your own.

2. Sit for a few moments and support yourself in accepting your fear. Most people do not do this. They try to skip over the fear and go directly into action, complaint, or denial because underneath the fear they feel helpless and alone.

There is nothing wrong with your fear. It does not weaken you or make you a less spiritual person, nor does it necessarily make you less effective in the world. In fact, fear carries strong energy that can be consciously directed into constructive thought and action. You can take advantage of this hidden power by giving yourself time to notice the fear. As long as it is there, go ahead and feel it. Let it have its expression. "So this is what it feels like to be afraid for my survival." Allow the fear to reveal itself.

3. Drop into a deeper level of self that is just underneath the fear. The fear may still be with you, but it is not all that exists. Along with the fear is something greater; it is the unconditional love and well-being of true self. Your breath can take you there instantly. Let each of your next ten breaths breathe you deeper into true self, gently and easily.

4. As your breath continues to take you deeper into true self, remember your connection with the planetary whole and its well-being. Everyone on the planet has a true self, and your true self is connected with everyone else's. Let your imagination show this to you. It may come to you as an image of being joined with everyone on the planet, or you may simple feel or sense the unity.

If you need to begin imagining this on a smaller, more personal scale, picture yourself in One mind with your friends or neighborhood. Perhaps you will find it easier to join with your town or your state or your country. The size of the group does not matter. Witnessing your connection in One mind with a small group is just as effective as witnessing it with the entire planet. One mind is One mind; no matter how you picture it, you are witnessing the connection you have with the entire world.

Sit for a few moments in the experience of One mind. It connects you with other people in love and in unlimited thought. Enjoy the aliveness and vitality of that connection.

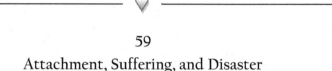

59
Attachment, Suffering, and Disaster

Many situations considered disasters by human beings are quite natural and necessary occurrences in the broader spectrum of nature. Floods, droughts, earthquakes, volcanic eruptions, fires, hurricanes, tornadoes, and other cataclysmic events have always occurred as the pulse and breath of our planet's evolution. Similarly, through violence, ecological blunders, and economic and political crises, humanity exhibits its extremes in its own struggles to evolve.

The higher collective consciousness, of which we are each a part, knows how important survival issues are for bringing the personality's awareness to the One mind, and thus disasters will continue to be part of human life for some time.

The most frightening thing about disaster is that it threatens our attachments. We tend to be attached to material things, to people, to being free of pain, to having certain feelings, to remaining alive, and to an array of other conditions. Of course, it isn't wrong to want these things. It is natural for the personality to seek safety, comfort, and companionship; the personality desires to be healthy and vital in every way possible. Yet desire and attachment are not always the same thing. If our sense of well-being is threatened when our desire is not fulfilled—or when we *fear* our desire may not be fulfilled—it is attachment.

Attachment is anything the personality
mistakes for true well-being.

Let's look at the most basic attachment: survival. Survival instinct tells you to stay alive at any cost. Attachment to staying alive, however, also includes the underlying belief that you will suffer in some way if you die. The aspect of personality that believes it will have well-being only as long as it stays physically alive is panicked at the thought of dying. To the degree you fear that death means losing your *true* well-being, you will be attached to physical survival.

This attachment will serve you by motivating you to make choices that will keep you alive. However, when it is time to die, this attachment will become a burden because it will cause your personality to fear death, and to feel anguish and suffering as death approaches. It will try to convince you that death is wrong and shouldn't happen. So instead of preparing you peacefully—and even joyfully—for the transition of death, it will make you feel conflict and distress.

Attachment to physical survival has only one gear, only one message it knows how to give: Avoid death at any cost. It has no awareness that there is a proper time to die or that there is an extraordinary well-being to be found in death.

On the other hand, if you know in every fiber of your being that unlimited spirit is what is most real in you—and that your spirit remains alive, vibrant, loving, and rooted in well-being after your physical death—the thought of dying will not bring you panic, pain, or suffering. You may still desire to stay physically alive and choose your daily actions accordingly, but you will not be under the control of attachment. You will be choosing life while not fearing death.

Attachments occur in all areas of our lives and can be difficult to discern. For example, you may have trouble recognizing attachment in a relationship because love and attachment are so easily entwined. You may feel the emotion of love but also, perhaps unconsciously, believe your well-being depends on that person. To the degree your well-being depends on another person, your relationship is replacing—and inadequately so—your relationship with true self and is an attachment.

Your relationship with true self (or Source, Spirit, God, the universe, All That Is—whatever term you prefer) is your primary relationship and the only one that can provide you with unwavering, unconditional well-being. Well-being is true self's nature. True self radiates well-being no matter what happens in your relationships or any other part of your life. True self's well-being is unconditional: It remains unwavering throughout all changes in the conditions of your life and the full range of your personality's feelings.

You may be tempted to say, "Well, it's okay to rely on people I love for my well-being because they are more important than material objects. Material things like money, cars, and houses have less spiritual value, but people are really important. So surely relying on people for my well-being can't be an attachment."

Yet, a dependency is a dependency, and you cannot "upgrade" by choosing a loftier one. Relying on a person, place, or event to replace the unconditional well-being of true self—or to compensate for your personality's disconnection from the unconditional well-being of true self—makes that reliance an attachment. The antidote to attachment is to open to true self and its well-being.

The more consciously you experience true self in your daily life,
the more unconditional well-being you feel.

Ironically, when you strengthen your experience of true self and integrate it into your life, you eventually will encounter a loss related to each of your attachments. Initially, as you allow the well-being of true self to fill your life, it radiates into your fears, loosening your personality's grip on attachments. Sometimes the process of releasing your attachments will be easy, giving you a deep sense of relief.

Other times it will be difficult and painful, stimulating the kind of fear and grief you had hoped all your life to avoid. Sooner or later in your return to true self each attachment will be challenged and relinquished. Yet you will discover that even those losses, no matter how much your personality feared them, do not disturb the deep, unwavering well-being in your true self. That is freedom.

Some people move through this process with outer dramas. They lose their homes in fires; they lose loved ones in accidents; they lose their jobs during a recession. They may do this sequentially, facing a new loss every few years, or they may do it all at once, losing everything in one disaster.

Other people go through the process of releasing their attachments internally, without manifesting much observable outer loss. For example, discord surfaces in their marriages, prompting a long, painful process of introspection. They learn to emotionally let go of their attachment to relationship as their primary source of well-being while they increase the well-being they receive from true self. Because of that shift, they work out their problems without losing their marriages—they just transform the attachment. Or shake-ups at work force them to stop relying on their jobs as their source of personal identity, but they do not end up actually losing their jobs.

Attachments distract the personality from unwavering well-being, diverting awareness away from our unlimited nature into limitation. A belief that our true well-being depends on having money, a home, a mate, a great car, nice clothes, or even good physical health reinforces the illusion that these limited things are the source of our existence and well-being.

Understand that there is nothing wrong with wanting those things, working for them, and enjoying them when we have them. It is our mistaking them for the source of our true well-being—or believing we can't have well-being without them—that makes them attachments.

Consider that your survival may depend solely
on your alignment with unlimited spirit.

The vital life force of unlimited spirit streaming through your body and your energy system is the cause of your existence. It is what gives you physical life and consciousness. It also carries the true joy and pleasure of being alive. No material thing or other physical being can give you the supreme happiness of conscious surrender to unlimited spirit as it carries you forward in the world. If you are out of touch with true self, fulfillment of your attachments will be a weak and temporary compensation, not a satisfying replacement.

There is no reason to feel bad about yourself for your attachment to externals. That's just part of your personality's way of relating to the physical world. Yet it can be helpful to witness your attachments and recognize them honestly for what they are: attempts to compensate for feeling separate from true self, or Source. This witnessing can make you uneasy because it brings your focus to the inner disconnection with which you have been living, and that is by nature uncomfortable. Still, it is helpful to witness this disconnection compassionately, staying with yourself and not turning away in spite of the discomfort or disorientation you may feel.

You long to be whole. You long to know the unconditional love and joy that is your true nature. If you feel separate and afraid—even secretly disappointed in life—it is important to recognize your disconnection from true self because that is essentially the cause of all your suffering.

All suffering is separation from Source.

Let's look at what this means in terms of your fears about survival. If one or more of your primary survival fears were to manifest, you would probably call it a disaster or a catastrophe. Losing your house and belongings in a flood could be one such event, and perhaps you fear it because of the suffering you would feel. Yet losing your home does not cause suffering; losing your home and not being aware of unlimited Source streaming through you causes the suffering.

Getting a debilitating or terminal disease is a common fear. Such an illness can certainly create physical and emotional pain, exhaustion, and ongoing distress. Yet, as uncomfortable as the illness may be, it is not the cause of suffering; illness without conscious experience of unlimited Source is the cause of suffering.

This is because pain is not necessarily suffering. Pain is simply pain—an intense sensation that is filtered through our consciousness, where it is interpreted according to our reality. We interpret pain as suffering only when we are not also aware of the unwavering well-being that exists, undisturbed, within us at a level deeper than the pain sensations.

In fact, living in any conditions without noticing the vibrant flow of Source and its unwavering well-being causes suffering. You can have an abundance of money, a beautiful home, excellent health, loving family and friends, and all the other "right" things and still suffer quietly and endlessly. Even though all your attachments are fulfilled, living without awareness of Source creates an inner disaster, and you are still suffering.

All people affect, and are affected by, each other through their participation in the collective consciousness. Because of this inherent connection, groups of people will act out the various survival issues of the whole planet to help bring growth and alignment to everyone on it. So, at different times and places, people will display, through their personalities, the planet's collective suffering that comes from the personality's lack of awareness of Source and its unwavering well-being. This will often be done through their participation in disasters.

You may witness these disasters because you live nearby, you know the people involved, or you see the disasters in the media. As a witness, you are in a sacred position. You are watching the display of an issue that connects you to those people no matter how far away they are. You are watching a situation that unfolds in part for your own growth, as well as for the contribution you can make back to the whole by your response.

When you see other people suffer, you witness their disconnection from Source. If seeing their suffering hurts you—or even causes you to criticize or judge them—it is because they reflect the pain of your own disconnection. This situation can be valuable if you let compassion open your heart to yourself and to your feelings. Then let compassion join you to the others who share your suffering and are displaying it for you.

60

From Crisis to Compassion

Responding to a disaster from compassion rather than from fear or crisis can be a tall order. Facing our disconnection from Source can seem overwhelmingly frightening. In fact, many people feel so threatened by their inner disconnection that they stay completely unconscious of it and don't let themselves feel it or deal with it at all. The result is that they automatically react to disaster, theirs or others', with instant fear or blame.

For most people, denial of the pain of disconnection is so strong that daily living is focused on attachments—external things, people, or specific situations—in an attempt to find happiness and security that would otherwise come from Source. This is a type of addiction. The suffering from this disconnection can be pushed so far into the unconscious that it takes the impact of a disaster to break through.

Disaster often causes the loss of one or more primary external attachments. It can jar people out of their pattern of addiction and force them to reevaluate their lives. For example, losing your home can force you to look at how deeply you relied on your possessions for your identity and security. You then have the opportunity to look within to find your true identity, recognizing that the external world reflects that identity to you but does not create it.

Similarly, losing your job or your life savings can force you to face questions about where you believe your true source of support exists and how fully you are able to trust it and rely on it. This inner inquiry can bring you to true self for support that is unconditional and cannot be lost.

Any event involving loss can trigger underlying panic and pain that comes from your personality's persistent attempts to maintain control in a world that is, in actuality, beyond its control. To "recover" you may need to surrender to an inner well-being that enriches your life regardless of external circumstances and then carefully re-create your life based on that surrender to inner well-being.

Losing loved ones, or even losing a relationship with them, can be the most trying disaster. All healing from this loss must be done with compassion and patience for yourself. Most close relationships are a combination of true, open-hearted love and the personality's attachment. Attachment—wanting the outer relationship to compensate for disconnection from true self—can be faced and used as a springboard to true self.

Some people who experience disaster are able to use it as a catalyst for freeing themselves of the attachment that is shaken loose. They let their lives be forever changed by that break in addiction. Seeing with a new focus, they learn to make choices that come from deeper truth. Others return to the addiction as soon as the outer crisis is over.

Whether you directly experience disaster or witness it elsewhere, you always have the opportunity to let the situation touch you and bring profound change into your life. You can allow the disaster to be a mirror, reflecting your inner disaster of living in disconnection from Source. Feel whatever emotions are present. Open to your suffering without turning away from it, *and* open to the unwavering love and well-being of Source. From there you have the power to make new choices and to create new possibilities.

Witnessing the suffering of others can be traumatic, even when the event is witnessed only though the media. Because of their difficulty coping with the trauma, witnesses often try to find order in the situation by making rationalizations or by passing judgment on the people who are the victims, or the cause, of the disaster. In an attempt to leap past their discomfort at being separated from Source, witnesses may react to the situation by saying such things as "Those people must have done something to deserve (or create) this." "Their way of living has been so out of balance that nature (or god) is teaching them a lesson." "Their bad luck (or bad karma) has made this happen to them." "Those people really don't feel things the way we do." "The people who caused this disaster are our enemies (or are evil)."

The list of possible judgments goes on endlessly and serves as a way of distancing ourselves from suffering. This is done automatically, and usually unconsciously, to avoid having the suffering of others remind us of our own distressing separation or trigger our inner suffering. Passing judgment is a very human thing to do, and it is not "wrong"; but it also is not helpful. It prevents us from going deeper into self where reconnection with Source can happen. (Note: No one is ever really disconnected from Source [true self]. The disconnection or separation discussed in this chapter is simply the personality's lack of conscious awareness of Source, which feels like a disconnection.)

If you notice yourself rationalizing, judging, or dismissing someone else's suffering, you can do something to gently nudge yourself out of this automatic, limited reaction.

ATTUNEMENT
Finding Compassion in a Crisis

1. Take a deep breath and give yourself a few quiet moments.

2. Recognize your judgment as a sign you need to have compassion for your deep, perhaps hidden suffering.

3. Let yourself experience the discomfort, to whatever degree it may be there, of feeling out of connection with true self, or Source. Feel the distress of missing it now. You may also feel the pain of having missed it at certain times in the past.

4. Let yourself feel how much you long for conscious experience of true self—the unlimited love and vitality of Source—streaming through your being, bringing you joy and well-being.

5. Gently take five to ten more breaths, imagining that each breath takes you a little deeper into your true self.

6. From that deeper place, allow the unlimited love of true self, which is the essence of your being, to flow through you, bringing comfort and connection.

61
Allowing Integration

Regardless of how you go through the process of loosening your grip on attachments and no matter how difficult it may be, letting go and turning your awareness toward true self opens you to greater possibilities. The inner emptiness you tried to fill with attachments eventually becomes spacious rather than vacant. It becomes an opening through which vibrant well-being can enter your life.

As you begin to live with new fulfillment, you may encounter some unexpected feelings of grief. Even though you may have a more expansive sense of self and feel a deeper love and joy, your personality may still need to grieve the loss of the attachments it had carried for so long. This is part of its adjustment to the new reality you are creating for yourself. So be aware that at times when you come into a profound expansiveness of being, there can also be a sense of loss. This feeling is quite natural. Feel the joy and feel the grief, too. Accept the full range of who you are in those moments.

Understand that your transformation may take you back and forth between seemingly opposite inner realities. For awhile you may live in the expansiveness of your true self: genuinely less attached to externals yet also very present in the world. You may relate to work, to people, and to material things from a place of deeper, unshakable love and well-being. Then, a few moments or days or weeks later, you may suddenly feel caught up in your old attachments again, as though you are not free of them after all. This process of cycling through one awareness to the other is part of the integration of newly learned experience. At such times have patience, stay present with yourself, and continue allowing your breath to return you to true self.

ATTUNEMENT
Witnessing Your Attachments

When facing your attachments, your first act of compassion for yourself is to allow the attachments to be there. Let the attachments be okay. You do not have to get over them. It is too much to expect yourself to notice attachments *and* get over them at the same time; your personality will resist that kind of pressure. You can, however, notice your attachments and give yourself permission to have them. That is compassionate witnessing.

Notice your attachments as they surface, and jot them down. This week you could probably make a list of ten or more things you are attached to. You may want to keep it on the refrigerator, like a shopping list, where it will be accessible. Give the list two columns, and use it the following way:

1. Each time you notice an attachment, write it down in the first column. There's no need to put in much description or explanation; you know what it is. Just name the attachment. For example, you might write,

Today I was attached to:
- *Money*
- *My child*
- *Getting my way at work*
- *Finding a relationship*
- *Eating sweets*

2. After you identify each attachment, use the second column to write what you were hoping to get from it. For "money" you may put "feeling safe" or "security". For "my child" you may have hoped for "feeling like I am a complete person". "Relationship" may have been meant to give you "validation that I am worthy of love and good things". Eating sweets may have been for "feeling comforted".

Allow yourself to list your attachments with acceptance. You are ready to look at them, which is the first step in releasing them. There's no need to be over your attachments by the end of the week. You just need to explore them. Be honest and forthright with yourself. You are giving yourself an important gift: awareness of the things that have been your substitute for Source.

RINCON

My second dog, Rincon, was down the hall in my bedroom, curled up and fast asleep on my bed. In the kitchen I was happily chopping vegetables for dinner while half-watching the news on my little counter top TV. Suddenly a chaotic chorus of screaming and shouting jolted me into looking up, where I saw image after image of helpless and flailing people being swooshed across the TV screen by the merciless tidal wave that was destroying their village. Most of them barely kept their heads above water; some of them went under, with little likelihood of resurfacing off camera.

I put down my knife and stepped back, as though the three feet of new distance might magically lessen the tragedy, or its impact on me.

The day before, along with the rest of the world, I had been shocked and saddened to learn of the devastating tsunami in the Indian Ocean. But tonight the real footage from inside the disaster was being televised. Clip after clip of it, mostly filmed by tourists lucky enough to be perched on the top floors and roofs of the tallest buildings, was being played nonstop.

Knowing about the tsunami and the lives lost was one thing, but hearing and seeing it happen, feeling so close that I wanted to reach out and yank those people out of the water and into my kitchen—that was another. Yesterday I had known what had happened; tonight I was *realizing* what had happened.

I don't know when I started crying, it was so soft and quiet. I only noticed my tears when I heard the faint thud of Rincon jumping off my bed, and then the poof, poof, poof of his big paws padding his way up the carpeted hall to the kitchen. There was no moment's wait at the doorway; he knew what he was doing. In three steps he was across the kitchen in front of me, his back to the TV and his soft, brown eyes looking calmly up at mine. More gracefully than I would expect from a 75-pound dog, he stretched up and planted his front paws on my shoulders. He broke eye contact only to reach his head forward and press a velvety cheek to mine, first against one side of my face, and then against the other. Then, as gently as he had approached, he pushed off and retraced his steps.

Still standing where Rincon had left me, my heart aching for the suffering I had witnessed on the other side of the world *and* comforted by the compassion I had just received in my kitchen, I heard the poof, poof, poof of Rincon's return down the hall, then his springy landing on the bed to curl up once more.

Part XI

YOU ARE THE EARTH

Living the One Body

62
Inner and Outer Realities

Our culture has traditionally maintained a strong division between inner experience and outer reality. In this separation, the personality has functioned under the assumption that our inner reality is only minimally related to outer reality. Primarily, we have believed that outer reality acts on us and that we respond. For example, we have taken for granted that outer occurrences—such as other people's words and actions, or events that happen around us or that we witness through media—cause our feelings and affect our thoughts.

We have experienced life this way through our personality. Yet, just beyond our personality's awareness a more intimate, reciprocal relationship between our inner self and outer reality has been flourishing. To see it, let's take another look at manifestation.

Your life manifests from your total sense of self. Your identity energetically emanates into the world, creating everything in your life and affecting your responses to it. This means that the inner you projects itself into the world and then interacts with its own projection. Essentially, you have been meeting manifestations of yourself every day.

This dynamic of manifestation has been going on forever, yet the cultural viewpoint has been that our inner experience does not directly affect our outer reality. Rather, it has assumed that outer reality can only be affected by our personal actions or by some other outer influence. The bottom line consistently has been a belief in two separate realities, rather than a unified one.

This separation of inner and outer realities has been valuable in supporting humanity's exploration of limitation. But now that the culture's consciousness is ready to go beyond the confines of life based on separation, something new is happening. The barrier of belief that has been keeping inner and outer realities separate is dissolving.

Much of the distress you see in the world comes from people living
as though everyone and everything they affect is not them.

People are willing to put up with all kinds of destruction as long as they believe it is not happening to them personally. This applies to your own life, too. For example, you may believe that the earth's resources are being depleted and that strip mining is one way it is happening. Although this issue may deeply concern you, you do not feel it with the immediacy you would feel, say, your foot being scraped. Yet the two events are variations of the same thing, and without the belief in separation you would feel them as such. Similarly, to the degree you are not fully aware that everything you do in your outer life is something you do to yourself, you contribute to the cultural belief in separation.

Again, now that the culture's consciousness is ready for change, the mass belief in separation is shifting. In a sense, the energetics of consciousness responsible for maintaining the clear division between inner and outer realities is losing its integrity. The old pattern can no longer be maintained. As the pattern transforms, the inner and outer realities begin to blend in humanity's awareness. It is as though these two realities, once separate, have now begun to flicker back and forth with each other. This will continue until there is no longer separation but a merging, a unity. Our awareness will be changed. Whatever we once thought existed externally will be recognized within us, too. And all that originates within us will be evident to us everywhere.

This is joyous news. It means that individually and collectively the culture can no longer hold separation in place. It can no longer deplete the earth without people consciously feeling the sensation in their own bodies and emotions. You may already be feeling some of this sensation. If you love the earth and feel pain about what is happening to it, you are in the awakening. It may be uncomfortable, but rejoice in your sensitivity. You are making an important connection.

As the inner and outer realities continue to merge, there is bound to be tremendous disorientation in people's lives across the planet. One place where this particularly shows up is in economics. In most cultures, use of money has been based on the belief in separation between inner and outer. People have thought of money as something separate from who they are within rather than a manifested expression or reflection of their essence and their current consciousness. They have seen money as something that exists completely outside them for the purpose of manipulating their outer conditions.

To the degree this is a culture's perspective, that culture's economy is shaken as the field of consciousness that has held the inner/outer separation in place transforms. Each culture's economy becomes unpredictable as the consciousness it reflects moves into a new way of being. None of these economies (or the world economy as a whole) is likely to stabilize until the cultural consciousness it reflects has stabilized into the new pattern of inner/outer unity.

The personality judges such economic changes as good or bad. It makes these judgments automatically and arbitrarily, based entirely on how comfortable or uncomfortable the situation is and on how much the change threatens the personality's attachments. If the economy takes a turn that causes distress, it is judged as bad. If it is a severe turn or an uncomfortable turn that stays for a long time, the personality's feelings of doom and fears about survival get highly activated and can seem very convincing.

The personality's reactions are to be respected, yet the self-compassionate thing to do is to *also* open our awareness to true self and its unwavering well-being and perception of perfection. We can then offer that unlimitedness to our personality while it is suffering in its limitation.

63

The World Catches Up with You

Allow yourself to observe the shift in your life as the separation between inner and outer realities weakens and dissolves. You may notice that it seems to be getting more difficult for you to close off from the world and the people in it. Perhaps you are more easily affected by what you observe in the world. At times you may feel as though all the pain and grief on the planet are closing in on you, and you are helpless in the midst of it. It becomes harder for your mind to keep telling you, "That is happening to other people. It doesn't have anything to do with me." Instead, you start thinking, "I never noticed before how bad things really are for so many people. It has never been this bad before, has it?"

The truth is that it *has* been this bad in one way or another for much of humanity's existence, but you are no longer able to keep yourself so separate from it. Now that you can no longer hold the belief in separation so strongly in place, you are more immersed in the world and more vulnerable to directly experiencing all that is manifested.

The world is becoming more personal to you.

What has always been *you* externally is becoming more real to you at an internal, personal level. Increasingly, you feel like you cannot get away from what is happening in the world. You might think this is because the recent, rapid fire technological advances keep putting you face to face with practically everything occurring across the globe. The internet, social networking, and telephone technology, for example, give you far more images and information than you can process.

Yet technology is not the reason you cannot distance yourself from the external world. In fact, technological advances that outwardly connect us with the world are happening *because* our consciousness is opening to the merging of inner and outer realities and to our true self connectedness with everyone and everything. As this shift in our consciousness speeds up, breakthroughs in the technologies that mirror our increasing awareness of connectedness will race forward even faster and with farther reaching results than anything we can imagine now.

The real reason you cannot distance yourself from the external world is because *all of it springs from within you in some way*. This means that you cannot make lasting change in the world by working exclusively to make the change "out there". Because outer reality springs from your conscious and unconscious experience of self, it forms itself to reflect *you*. If you want to live in a world greatly changed from what you now see, view the world as a reflection of what you carry within. Let the outer world take you back to its source of creation, your inner self. That is the place to begin transformation.

Many people try to hold the outer world out. They see what is "wrong" out there and try hard to fix it. But all the while they keep their faces turned from themselves. The world cannot be fixed that way. In fact, the world cannot be fixed at all. Rather, as you let the world back into your heart, back into your being, it will graciously transform.

64
Healing the World

You may already be working on this transformation in your own way. Opening to yourself is the key. When you allow your deep, personal issues of distress, and even emotional or physical abuse, to surface and be acknowledged, felt, and shared with understanding and supportive people, you are healing yourself and the world. You are bringing to awareness the distressing inner experiences you have been unconsciously emanating into the world. Just as the energy of those inner conflicts has been repeating the experience of distress or abuse within your system all this time, it has been contributing to the manifestation of distress and abuse in the world. As you bring healing to yourself, you are offering healing to the world.

It may be uncomfortable to hear that issues you have been carrying internally, and probably unconsciously, have been "contributing to the distress and abuse in the world". If so, take a deep breath and let yourself be aware that this does not mean there is anything wrong with you. It also does not mean you are necessarily responsible for anyone else's suffering, violence, or misdirected action. It simply means that the inner reality you have been carrying has contributed to the cultural and planetary consciousness that has manifested those things.

You are part of the creation of everything
that exists in the world.

It is important to recognize this great influence your inner reality has on the outer world. When you turn away from it, insisting that what happens "out there" is caused "out there," you keep yourself disconnected from your greatest power for creating change: yourself. Nothing can manifest in your outer reality that does not reflect some part of you. As you compassionately own your connection to what is manifested, you reconnect with yourself at a level where you can make meaningful change both internally and externally.

Let's look at an example. We have already discussed how your personality fears its own destruction because it does not recognize as real the unlimited life and unwavering well-being that exists in pure spirit. Therefore, you are carrying fears and beliefs that you can be destroyed. The energy patterns of those fears and beliefs about your destruction emanate into the world where they manifest "out there" in situations that seem to occur independently of you. The possibility of the planet's destruction is a manifestation of this personal issue on a grand scale.

There are innumerable actions you can take to try to prevent the planet's destruction. You can try to change other people's behavior as well as your own. You can try to change people's priorities and ways of looking at how their actions affect the world. Noticeable progress can be made from these efforts, but unless the inner issue also changes, the outer progress will routinely suffer significant setbacks. As long as the inner issue of your own destruction is active, the outer issue of destruction will continue to be expressed in the world.

Facing this outer issue as a reflection of an inner issue gives you the opportunity to make peace in the most powerful place first: within yourself. As you turn inward and your personality speaks to you about its vulnerability and fear—showing you the emotions, beliefs, and personal history that have been causing its distress—you can compassionately witness its reality. If you do not want to be limited to that reality, within yourself and in the world, you can add the unlimitedness of true self to it.

To make that choice, remember the love that you are and the love that is the essence of all things and all beings. Imagine that you inhale unwavering compassion, support, and healing. Gently open to the vibrant flow of life force that is unthreatened and undiminished by any thoughts, feelings, or events. As you do this, you bring unlimitedness (unlimited love, compassion, support, healing, and life force) alongside limitation (the personality's fears and beliefs in its destruction).

Remember that unlimitedness carries greater essential truth than does limitation—and when you carry both in your awareness, the former will affect the latter. As the alignment you hold with unlimitedness begins to teach and repattern your personality's limitation, your experience of self will become more expansive. The energy patterns your consciousness emanates into the world will reflect that new expansiveness and will be your contribution to the collective consciousness.

Through repeatedly bringing unlimitedness into your *inner* experience of what is manifested in the world, you will start relating more to your spiritual indestructibility than to your personality's fears of physical destruction. And your thoughts, feelings, and actions will increasingly spring from unlimited love and unwavering well-being.

The collective consciousness manifests world events and situations. Because you are part of the collective consciousness, your expanded awareness will contribute to the creation of tangible global conditions that reflect unlimited love and unwavering well-being. Others who are taking practical action to create these conditions will also be supported by your energy.

With this in mind, let's review the main steps for using the power of inner connection to deal with world issues that distress you.

ATTUNEMENT
Responding to Distress in the World

1. Let any distressing issue in the world you take your awareness to your inner version of that issue.

2. Gently explore that inner issue as it relates to your personal life—

LOUISA

"The Nothing is everything," answered Louisa when I asked to hear her most important true self lesson. "Going into the space in myself that seems like nothing is where I find who I really am. What appears to be darkness and nothingness turns out to be all potential."

"How did you discover that?" I asked, wondering why I didn't know the answer. Friends for twenty years, we had shared so many of the struggles and triumphs in our lives that I was surprised not to remember this spiritual milestone of hers.

"In the late eighties, I was having a problem in my meditations—or at least I thought it was a problem," she began. "After closing my eyes and settling in, I would find myself facing a big hole of darkness. 'There's nothing there,' I would think, 'What do I do with this big hole of dark nothing?' My impulse was to reject it and search for the uplifting experiences I was used to in meditation, but the dark hole kept appearing. I was sure something was wrong. I hadn't started meditation to find darkness!"

No wonder I didn't recollect this story; Louisa and I had only begun to get to know each other then. Neither of us had yet recognized what good friends we would become or how long lasting our friendship would be. "What kind of meditation were you doing back then?" I inquired.

"I had learned a meditation practice of closing my eyes, silently saying, 'Relax, relax, relax,' and then continuing to sit quietly. It was wonderful. Not only did I feel relaxed during the meditation, I felt uplifted, light, buoyant, and deeply at ease. My daily concerns—work, money, relationships—faded, becoming less important to my well-being. Daily struggle fell away. I felt expanded, and my greater being became more real to me.

"Then, one day it changed. The darkness and nothingness started appearing. Almost as soon as I closed my eyes it was right in front of me. I couldn't see beyond it or get past it. 'I know there's more to me than this,' I thought, 'where is it?' I assumed something was wrong—perhaps I was feel the feelings, observe the beliefs, and share your heartfelt experience with trusted support people.

3. As you accept the existence of the inner limitation, invite unlimitedness in, too. You can let your breath breathe you into true self, take a few minutes for prayer or meditation, or use another technique you prefer.

4. Imagine your new focus on unlimitedness bringing love and well-being into your life and expanding your perceptions of yourself, others, and the world.

5. From this alignment with unlimited love and well-being, take the outer action toward creating a healthier world that feels genuinely right to you. Remember this inner alignment as you take that action.

65

Sharing Consciousness with the Earth

It's true what they say: The earth *is* your mother. This image is not just poetic; it is true at an essence level. The vibrational pattern of your body matches the vibrational pattern of the earth, which means that you and the earth share consciousness. The earth affects you, and you affect it.

Not only do you take in energy directly from the earth, but it also takes in energy from you. Whatever is going on in your body is energetically projected outward, and the earth receives it. Because the personality lives in your body, your issues about abuse and beliefs about your destructibility are projected out to the earth, contributing to its vulnerability to these same experiences of abuse and destruction.

You cannot stop the natural emanation of your energy patterns to the earth any more than you can keep air from leaving your lungs as you exhale. It will not help to try to control the process by thinking, "I'm not going to project any negativity or destruction into the world." Such resistance to yourself will only create more energy of conflict and struggle, which also will emanate outward.

Instead, accept the connection you have with the earth and take care of yourself and the earth together. You can begin the process by becoming conscious of your inner issues. Accept that the energy of those issues connects you to the outer world in every moment. To whatever degree is healthy and appropriate for you, gently face experiences you still carry that, at some point in your past, might have seemed threatening to your emotional or physical survival. You may discover forgotten instances of abandonment, neglect, or abuse. Open your heart to yourself as you explore, and get support from others—including a therapist or other type of counselor if you need to.

Don't give up on yourself. As you heal yourself you are healing the earth. Because your healing and the earth's healing are one, whenever you want greater healing for the earth, gently and compassionately go into the places within yourself that need healing. The heart of your work is there.

Finding inner healing may include accepting feelings of fear or anguish you have avoided all your life. It may require learning to receive love you never thought you deserved, or to forgive where you never thought forgiveness was possible. As you surrender to your healing, you come to a depth of connection with who you truly are that reminds you that the greatest truth is, and always has been, unwavering perfection and well-being. You have the opportunity to embody this truth as you open your heart in compassion to your personality's limitation and suffering and open your mind to your deep memory of unlimited being.

From unlimited spirit's perspective,
perfection is all that has ever existed,
and it is all that exists now.

Our journey Home is our movement into full awareness of this perfection. As we attune our inner hearing to the whispers of true self, we move forward on a path of profound exploration. By giving love to ourselves and each other, we generate the light that reveals each step along the way.

Part XII

MY STORY: EPILOGUE

My Life Goes to the Dogs

66
Lessons of New Love

Living from true self opens us to ever-deepening layers of unconditional love our personality doesn't know we carry. No matter how many times it has happened before, each new discovery of love is a surprise, something we didn't see coming and couldn't have predicted. Because our personality is outer focused, it often attributes the cause of the new love to a person or circumstance in our outer life. "The person I'm dating is so wonderful that I'm in love like never before." "My new job is a dream come true. The environment is so supportive that I feel really good about myself and other people."

People and circumstances can be catalysts for us to open more deeply to ourselves, but they are not the cause of love. When we observe new love as it emerges within us, we can recognize it as the same love it has always been, *the love that we are*, flowing through circuits of our personality's awareness for the first time.

We have galaxies of worlds within us.
Each time our personality opens to
the love that we are in a new way,
one of those worlds opens to us.

In 2002, a new love emerged within me so powerfully that another world opened—one I had paid only faint attention to and had always kept at a distance. It was the world of dogs.

I know, dog lovers are saying, "Whaa-at? How could you have been distant from dogs? That doesn't even make sense."

Since college I had been a cat person and considered my cats cherished family members. In contrast, I had felt little connection with dogs and preferred them at a distance. Their behavior at close range—the jumping, drooling, and dirty paws—was too much for me.

Then one Saturday afternoon, in a split second, that all changed. I fell passionately and irrevocably in love with dogs.

There wasn't even a dog in sight when it happened. I was getting my hair cut when I overheard the woman in the next chair telling her stylist about her dog. She had gotten him as a puppy from a local organization that provided assistance dogs to people with disabilities. As a volunteer puppy raiser, it had been her job to raise and train him for a year, and then to give him back to the organization for his advanced training and possible placement as a working dog for someone living with a disability. Her year with him was almost up.

I was half-listening, not paying attention to her details, when a lightning strike of energy surged through my body and snapped me into clear focus. I *knew*, I absolutely *knew*, that now I loved dogs and that I was to become a puppy raiser like her.

The assistance dog organization was closed for the weekend, and waiting for Monday was worse than the longest wait for Christmas I had ever suffered as a child. Love for dogs filled my heart and my thoughts constantly. I wanted my dog *now*. I couldn't believe I had lived so long without dogs—and that I hadn't missed them! Suddenly all dogs were beautiful to me, and I longed to be close to them.

Monday finally arrived, and I applied. Soon I was matched with my puppy, Chloe, a yellow Labrador and Golden Retriever mix who became the center of my life. For the next year we attended dog training classes and were together almost 24 hours a day. Because she was in training to become a service dog, she was permitted everywhere with me—stores, movies, restaurants, art shows, public transportation—and her manners became impeccable in all situations. She stuck by my side in supermarkets, and when I had to dash back to the last aisle for an item I had forgotten, she lay quietly next to our cart, out of the way of other shoppers, until I returned.

I had always heard people say that the marvelous thing about dogs is that they love us unconditionally. No one had ever told me that an even more powerful and healing force is the unconditional love *we feel for our dogs*. Whenever I looked at Chloe, or even thought of her, I felt the pure, unconditional love of true self radiating through me. Because she was with me all day, that was a lot of unconditional love!

67
Dog Training as a Spiritual Practice

Chloe loved training and, to my great surprise and delight, I discovered I was a natural at it. For both of us, training was a series of fun games that built our relationship and brought us joy. I didn't think about it at the time, but dog training became the perfect exercise for integrating my personality and true self: the conditional and the unconditional.

Training dogs is rooted in the conditional: We teach dogs to behave to specifications that change according to conditions. When they're on leash, they are to greet people and other dogs calmly and appropriately; when they're off leash at the dog park, they can run around and jump on each other in play. Yet our *relationship* with dogs is based in unconditional love: We love our dogs in all situations, no matter how the conditions change.

To do well with dogs, we must adapt our training to changing conditions
while remaining in the unconditionally loving state.
Our tactics change; our love does not.

As it turns out, this is also the formula for success in our relationship with our self and our relationships with other people. Our emotions and behaviors change according to changing conditions, but deeper, unconditional love remains constant. This is a challenging formula for the personality to apply. The personality has trouble discerning the changing, conditional emotion of love from true self's unconditional love.

Conditional emotions come and go in reaction to changes in conditions. For example, when people we love are good to us, our personality feels love for them. Then, when those same people are mean to us, that is a change in conditions; and the love disappears as our pain or anger arises. That kind of love, pain, and anger is conditional.

Yet even if we don't consciously notice it, underneath those emotions the unwavering, unconditional love we are made of continues radiating to those people—and to our self. The more adept we become at noticing that constant radiance of unconditional love, the more balanced and stable we become, regardless of what direction the winds of emotion are blowing.

Dog lovers know that a profound love bonds us with our dog. But when our dog still won't come after we've called 10 times, chews an expensive shoe, or toilets in the house *again*, our personality might suddenly feel frustrated or angry instead of loving. The personality's emotions are volatile as conditions change. Yet the more conscious we become of the unconditional love that keeps flowing, undisturbed, below the surface of that volatility, the more relaxed and patient we naturally remain with our dog.

> *True self's unconditional love is not an emotion,*
> *but a state of being. It is quieter, more subtle,*
> *and more enduring than emotion.*

With practice, I learned to remain tethered to my unconditional love no matter what Chloe was doing or which of my emotions surfaced. To be a good dog trainer, I also had to stay present in the moment and—this surprised me—let my conditional emotions become *even more conditional*. I had to learn not to hold onto emotions but to *let them go the moment the conditions that had triggered them changed.*

For example, in the early days it was hard to get Chloe to sit when guests came through the front door and she wanted to dash over and jump on them. Sometimes I felt exasperated because it took such effort to get her attention. But the moment she finally looked at me and placed her little butt on the floor, I praised her and let all my exasperation immediately disappear. The moment the condition (Chloe not sitting) changed, my conditional emotion (the exasperation that went with that condition) had to change, too.

If I had not learned to let my conditional emotions go, I would have been a poor trainer. Chloe would have heard me say *Good sit!* in a happy voice, but internally I would have been feeling exasperation spill-over: *Well, that's good you're sitting now, but you sure took long enough and I didn't know if it was ever going to happen. It's so frustrating when we go through this, and we go through this every day! Sheesh, how long is it going to take for us to get good at this?*

Because dogs respond to our emotions even more than to our words, Chloe would have felt my exasperation linger as she was sitting for me. That mixed message—*Good sit* and *I'm still unhappy with you*—would have confused her and taken the fun out of sitting for me. Then she would have felt even less motivated to sit for me the next time.

How many times have we all held onto conditional emotions after the conditions had changed? Long after someone gave us a genuine apology, we still ran their offense through our minds, telling our self and our friends the story again and again, feeling our original hurt or outrage each time. Or we fell short of our own expectations in a situation and, even years later, continued to feel bad about it.

Conditional emotions are *meant* to come and go with changing conditions. If we do not let them go as conditions change, we interfere with their naturally brief lives. Replaying them hours, weeks, months, or years later keeps them on an artificial, mental life support system for a period that is outrageously beyond their intended life span. Doing that throws us off balance and reduces our presence with whatever is genuinely occurring in the now.

So I learned—initially because it got better results from my dog, but later because I realized it was a life lesson—to drop my discomfort the second the unsettling condition changed. That is a lesson I continue to practice as much as I can.

When we're learning to open to true self, it can be a relief to realize that our personality's conditional emotions do not need to control us or interfere with our well-being. We can manage them in two simple ways:

1. While we're feeling the emotion, remember that we have a deeper, unconditional love radiating within us that is our tether to equanimity.

2. Let go of the uncomfortable emotion the moment the condition that triggered it changes.

68

Conditions Change Again

Too soon, my year with Chloe was up and I had to give her back to the assistance dog organization. I was unprepared for the loss. Day after day, my house and car seemed unbearably empty. As I rolled my cart up and down the aisles of the grocery store, I felt like half of me was missing. And sadly, I didn't think I could ever love another dog.

For three weeks I moped, hardly leaving my house, feeling *Why go anywhere without my dog?* Then everything changed. I was offered another dog, a one-year old named Rincon (also a yellow Labrador and Golden Retriever). Within hours of picking him up, I knew we were a wonderful match. He was just the nicest guy you'll ever meet—and he loved training. The best part was that I got to keep him.

Rincon showed me I *could* love another dog after Chloe—and many other dogs, too! After he and I had mastered all the dog training I knew, we learned Canine Freestyle Dance (often called *dog dancing*—people and their dogs doing fun dance steps together). My love of dogs kept growing, so I started a side business called Hot Diggity Dog! where Rincon and I teach dog training and dog dancing. Rincon is the sweetest business partner I have ever had, and every dog we work with makes me happy.

Once again, true self has opened a new world to me that I never could have imagined or predicted—or even known I had wanted! It had been off the map of my personality's limited awareness until I stepped into it. Now it's a world where unconditional love radiates through me and I feel joy every day.

69
Smooth Sailing

Not everything I've wanted in my life has worked out, and some things that *have* worked out have seemed to take forever, with endless stops and starts along the way. Yet, with dogs it has been smooth sailing from the moment I fell in love with them back in that hair salon.

Why has the world of dogs opened to me so easily and richly? Perhaps the answer takes us back to the unconditional love mentioned in the beginning of this chapter. I think that in 2002 my personality was opening to a deeper layer of unconditional love within me, and the moment of breakthrough was that lightning strike of love I felt at the salon. From there, it's easy to understand how dogs would be a perfect match to the vibration of unconditional love—and perfect partners for me to practice the lessons of love that came with it.

As we know, the personality might be tempted to attribute that love to an external source and say that I fell in love with dogs because *they* are so unconditionally loving and wonderful. Yet, as wonderful as dogs are, if *I* love dogs, my love originates within me.

My true self mentoring and classes are still my central focus, but I have learned that there are always rich and rewarding adventures waiting for us that we cannot see yet. For me, true self channeling, sounding, painting, and dogs are proof of that. Each has taught me that there is no limit to the love we carry or to the ways it can emerge.

No matter who or what is wonderful in our lives, our love always originates within us—because that love is what we *are made of.* It is our essence, our source, our true self, and it is always gently yet powerfully waiting to open new worlds for us.

CONTACT

Find out more about Martia Nelson's True Self™ Mentoring programs for individuals and groups. She offers special tracks for motivated business owners and professionals who want high level business success, spiritual awakening and juicy, joyful lives—or who feel a deeper life purpose calling.

Martia is a vibrant speaker who deeply touches and motivates audiences of all sizes.

Martia Nelson
P.O. Box 1932
Sebastopol, CA 95473
martia@sonic.net
www.MartiaNelson.com   Get your free gift.

Martia and Rincon's dog training:
Hot Diggity Dog!
www.DogDancer.com   See the fun video clip.

Martia's nonprofit art project to support people coping with cancer:
Arts for Healing
www.ArtsforHealing.com   See beautiful art.

NOTES

52215811R00173

Made in the USA
San Bernardino, CA
15 August 2017